Old Testament Readings & Devotionals Volume 1

Old Testament Readings & Devotionals Volume 1

With

R. Hawker

C. H. Spurgeon

O. Winslow

Compiled by C. M. H. Koenig

Old Testament Readings & Devotionals

Volume 1

Published by
Inscript Books
A Division of Dove Christian Publishers
P.O. Box 611
Bladensburg, MD 20710-0611
www.inscriptpublishing.com

Cataloging-in-Publication Data
Names: Koenig, C.M.H., compiler. | Hawker, Robert, 1753-1827, author. | Spurgeon, C. H. (Charles Haddon), 1834-1892, author. | Winslow, Octavius, -1878, author.
Title: Old Testament readings & devotions, volume 1 / C.M.H. Koenig, compiler.
Description: Bladensburg, MD : Inscript Books, 2020. | Also available in ebook format.
Identifiers: LCCN 2020939877 (print) | ISBN 978-1-7348625-5-3 (paperback)
Subjects: LCSH: Bible. Old Testament. | Bible. Old Testament--Devotional literature. | Bible. Genesis. | Bible. Job. | Bible. Psalms. | Spiritual life--Christianity. | BISAC: RELIGION / Christian Living / Devotional. | RELIGION / Biblical Studies / Old Testament / General.
Classification: LCC BS1151.55 .O43 2020 (print) | LCC BS1151.55 (ebook) | DDC 221.6--dc23.

Printed in the United States of America

Preface

This work is the first of fourteen (14) volumes, which combines a chronological reading plan of the Bible with a related devotional for each "reading." Each reading is generally one chapter and the associated devotionals are excerpts from Robert Hawker (1753–1827), Charles H. Spurgeon (1834-1892), or Octavius Winslow's (1808-1878) works. There are eleven (11) volumes for the Old Testament and three (3) volumes for the New Testament. The Old Testament volumes average about 79 days' worth of readings each. The New Testament volumes average about 86 days' worth of readings each. The Psalms are interspersed throughout the Old Testament volumes.

The intent of the series is to help us savor the scriptures and, in the words of the Psalmist, to "Taste and see that the LORD is good" (Psalm 34:8, CSB).

"Charles Spurgeon commended Robert Hawker with these words: "Gentleman, if you want something full of marrow and fatness, cheering to your own hearts by way of comment, and likely to help you in giving your hearers rich expositions, buy Dr. Hawker's Poor Man's Commentary. ... he sees Jesus, and that is a sacred gift, which is most precious whether the owner be a critic or no. There is always such a savor of the Lord Jesus Christ in Dr. Hawker that you cannot read him without profit.""

Unless otherwise noted, the key verse(s) for each day (in italics) are from the Christian Standard Bible (CSB).

Contents and Reading Chart

Day 1

Reading: Genesis 1

"God saw that the light was good, and God separated the light from the darkness." Genesis 1:4

Light might well be good since it sprang from that fiat of goodness, "Let there be light." We who enjoy it should be more grateful for it than we are, and see more of God in it and by it. Light physical is said by Solomon to be sweet, but gospel light is infinitely more precious, for it reveals eternal things, and ministers to our immortal natures. When the Holy Spirit gives us spiritual light, and opens our eyes to behold the glory of God in the face of Jesus Christ, we behold sin in its true colors, and ourselves in our real position; we see the Most Holy God as he reveals himself, the plan of mercy as he propounds it, and the world to come as the Word describes it. Spiritual light has many beams and prismatic colors, but whether they be knowledge, joy, holiness, or life, all are divinely good. If the light received be thus good, what must the essential light be, and how glorious must be the place where he reveals himself. O Lord, since light is so good, give us more of it, and more of thyself, the true light.

No sooner is there a good thing in the world, than a division is necessary. Light and darkness have no communion; God has divided them, let us not confound them. Sons of light must not have fellowship with deeds, doctrines, or deceits of darkness. The children of the day must be sober, honest, and bold in their Lord's work, leaving the works of darkness to those who shall dwell in it for ever. Our Churches should by discipline divide the light from the darkness, and we should by our distinct separation from the world do the same. In judgment, in action, in hearing, in teaching, in association, we must discern between the precious and the vile, and maintain the great distinction which the Lord made upon the world's first day. O Lord Jesus, be thou our light throughout the whole of this day, for thy light is the light of men. (Spurgeon, Morning, Jan 5)

Reading: Genesis 2

"Then the LORD God formed the man out of the dust from the ground and breathed the breath of life into his nostrils ..." Genesis 2:7

Many are the sweet reflections which are suggested to the Reader's mind, from the perusal of this Chapter. Here is the first institution of the holy sabbath. And here we meet also with the first institution of the holy estate of marriage. Both of divine authority. Both sanctioned by God himself; and therefore, both worthy to be observed with suitable reverence. Concerning the *former*, I would say to the pious Reader, may it be your mercy, and mine, to honor the Lord's day, on account of the many precious purposes, for which the Lord himself honored it: and *to cease from our own works, as God did from His.* And concerning the *latter*, I would add a prayer, that a due sense of the Divine appointment, in the institution of holy wedlock, may make every one engaged in it, remember what the Apostle says: *Marriage is honorable unto all, and the bed undefiled; but whoremongers and adulterers God will judge.* But doth not the idea of union in the marriage-state, in this life, awaken a spiritual improvement, and call up to the recollection of the true believer in Jesus, the sweet thought of our spiritual union with Him, who hath betrothed his people to himself, forever?

Oh! what a precious scripture is that; *Thy Maker is thy Husband; the Lord of Hosts is his name.*[1] Dearest Jesus, be Thou my Husband, Shepherd, Friend!

May the recollection, which the 7th verse of this chapter awakens, of the dust of which our nature was formed, remind you and me of our earthly extraction; so that we can truly say to *corruption, thou art my father; and to the worm, thou art my mother and my sister.*[2] But at the same time, may the pleasing thought, that the LORD God hath breathed into our nostrils the breath of life, make us never forget our heavenly relationship. And oh! that God the Holy Spirit would breathe upon the dry bones, both of him that writes and him that reads, and bid us live.

Reader! do not overlook the very gracious doctrine of the 20th verse. *There was not found an help meet for Adam.* No! There is not, there cannot be, in any, or in all the creatures of God's providence, an help meet. And though the LORD God brought the woman to our first father, as a suitable help meet for the *body*; yet it is the *Seed of the Woman*, alone, which can become an Help-meet for the *soul*. Dearest Jesus! be thou my Help, my Hope, and my Portion forever. (Hawker, Poor Man's Old Testament Commentary: Genesis-Numbers, 13-14)

---

1   Isaiah 54:5
2   Job 17:14

Reading: Genesis 3

"... the voice of the Lord God walking in the garden in the cool of the day ..." Genesis 3:8 (AKJV)

My soul, now that the cool of the day has come, retire awhile and hearken to the voice of thy God. He is always ready to speak with thee when thou art prepared to hear. If there be any slowness to commune it is not on his part, but altogether on thine own, for he stands at the door and knocks, and if his people will but open, he rejoices to enter. But in what state is my heart, which is my Lord's garden? May I venture to hope that it is well trimmed and watered, and is bringing forth fruit fit for him? If not, he will have much to reprove, but still I pray him to come unto me, for nothing can so certainly bring my heart into a right condition as the presence of the Sun of Righteousness, who brings healing in his wings. Come, therefore, O Lord, my God, my soul invites thee earnestly, and waits for thee eagerly. Come to me, O Jesus, my well-beloved, and plant fresh flowers in my garden, such as I see blooming in such perfection in thy matchless character! Come, O my Father, who art the Husbandman, and deal with me in thy tenderness and prudence! Come, O Holy Spirit, and bedew my whole nature, as the herbs are now moistened with the evening dews. O that God would speak to me. Speak, Lord, for thy servant heareth! O that he would walk with me; I am ready to give up my whole heart and mind to him, and every other thought is hushed. I am only asking what he delights to give. I am sure that he will condescend to have fellowship with me, for he has given me his Holy Spirit to abide with me forever. Sweet is the cool twilight, when every star seems like the eye of heaven, and the cool wind is as the breath of celestial love. My Father, my elder Brother, my sweet Comforter, speak now in lovingkindness, for thou hast opened mine ear and I am not rebellious. (Spurgeon, Eve, Jul 1)

Reading: Genesis 4

"... Abel became a shepherd of flocks ..." Genesis 4:2

*A*s a shepherd Abel *sanctified his work to the glory of God, and offered a sacrifice of blood upon his altar, and the Lord had respect unto Abel and his offering.* This early type of our Lord is exceedingly clear and distinct. Like the first streak of light which tinges the east at sunrise, it does not reveal everything, but it clearly manifests the great fact that the sun is coming. As we see Abel, a shepherd and yet a priest, offering a sacrifice of sweet smell unto God, we discern our Lord, who brings before his Father a sacrifice to which Jehovah ever hath respect. Abel was hated by his brother—hated without a cause; and even so was the Savior: the natural and carnal man hated the accepted man in whom the Spirit of grace was found, and rested not until his blood had been shed. Abel fell, and sprinkled his altar and sacrifice with his own blood, and therein sets forth the Lord Jesus slain by the enmity of man while serving as a priest before the Lord. "The good Shepherd layeth down his life for the sheep."[3] Let us weep over him as we view him slain by the hatred of mankind, staining the horns of his altar with his own blood. *Abel's blood speaketh.* "The Lord said unto Cain, 'The voice of thy brother's blood crieth unto me from the

3　　John 10:11

ground.'" The blood of Jesus hath a mighty tongue, and the import of its prevailing cry is not vengeance but mercy. It is precious beyond all preciousness to stand at the altar of our good Shepherd! to see him bleeding there as the slaughtered priest, and then to hear his blood speaking peace to all his flock, peace in our conscience, peace between Jew and Gentile, peace between man and his offended Maker, peace all down the ages of eternity for blood-washed men. Abel is the first shepherd in order of time, but our hearts shall ever place Jesus first in order of excellence. Thou great Keeper of the sheep, we the people of thy pasture bless thee with our whole hearts when we see thee slain for us. (Spurgeon, Morning, Jan 20)

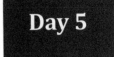

Reading: Genesis 5

"... Enoch walked with God ..." Genesis 5:22

I have often considered, and as often found pleasure, in the consideration of the very honorable testimony which the Holy Spirit hath given to the faith of the patriarchs, both in the Old and New Testaments. What wonders were wrought by faith! "They walked with God! They endured (saith the sacred writer) as seeing him who is invisible."[4] They communed with God, and were as conscious of his spiritual presence, and spiritual society, as we are of sensible objects. Hence, by these acts of frequent communion, the souls found a growing likeness. The more they loved God, the more their minds were led by grace into an increasing conformity to what they loved. This assimilation is a natural consequence, even among natural things. He that walketh with wise men will be wise. We naturally imbibe the manners, the sentiments, yea, the very habits, of those with whom we like to associate. How much more must a frequent intercourse and communion with the Lord, and under his spiritual teaching, induce a conformity to the most fair, most lovely, and most beloved object of the soul! "Beholding, (saith the Apostle.) as in a glass, the glory of the Lord, we are changed into the same image, from glory to glory, even as by the

---

4   Hebrews 11:27

Spirit of the Lord."[5] Are these things so? Then it is explained to thee, my soul, wherefore it is that thou goest so lean, and art yet so poor in the divine life. Thou dost not, as Enoch did, keep up a continual communion with Jesus. Pause, this evening, over the subject, and see if this be not the case. All the days of thine unregeneracy, before thou wert first brought acquainted with God in Christ, were spent in a total ignorance of God. There was then no communion with him; yea, not even the desire of communion. But when God, who commanded the light to shine out of darkness, shined into thine heart, then was first given to thee the light of the knowledge of the glory of God, in the face of Jesus Christ. Recollect, then, what were thy feelings when the day-spring from on high first visited thee. Didst thou not flee to Jesus, as the man-slayer hastening for his life to the city of refuge? Oh! how feelingly wert thou made to value the very name of a Savior! How earnestly didst thou seek him above thy necessary food! And if thou hast since intermitted those visits to Jesus, and lost a sense of thy daily want of him, can it be a subject of wonder that this leanness of soul is induced in thee? Will not a distance from, and a shyness of, Jesus, produce a poverty in spiritual things, as much as the want of food to the body will bring on a leanness and a decline in bodily things? Learn, then, this evening, an unanswerable reply to all thy complaints, and the complaints of the Church at large. Wherefore is it that believers live so much below their privileges, but because they live so much below the enjoyment of sweet communion with Jesus? If worldly concerns

5   2 Corinthians 3:18

swallow up our time, as the earth did Korah and his company; if we are satisfied with a mere form of prayer in our morning and evening retirement, and in our family worship before God, while destitute of the power of godliness; if we are still but little acquainted with the Lord, and seldom go to court to behold the king in his beauty, and to be favored with his smiles; it is no longer a matter of surprise, that, from keeping so poor a house, we are so poor in enjoyment. Oh! for grace to walk with God, as Enoch walked! Make me, thou dear Lord, jealous above all things of my own heart. Let every morning, with the first dawn of day, call me up to holy communion with thee. And let every night toll the bell of reflection, to examine what visits I have had *from* thee, and what visits I have made *to* thee; and let nothing satisfy my soul but the continual walk of faith with thee; that from an increasing knowledge *of* thee, increasing communion *with* thee, and increasing confidence *in* thee, my soul may be growing up into such lively actings of grace upon thy person, blood, and righteousness, that a daily walk of communion with my Lord may be gradually preparing my soul for the everlasting enjoyment of him; and when death comes, though it make a change of place, yet will it make no change of company; but "awaking up after thy likeness, I shall be fully satisfied with it." (Hawker, The Poor Man's Evening Portion, Jan 13)

Day 6

Reading: Genesis 6

""... for I regret that I made them." Noah, however, found favor with the LORD." Genesis 6:7-8

What dreadful consequences of the guilt related in this chapter, soon followed ungracious and unholy connections in the marriage state, between the seed of Seth and the seed of Cain! What sad events is sin ever producing in private life, and in public bodies! How hath it drawn away the wisest of men to idolatry! See 1 Kings 11:1, 4. How hath it corrupted the church itself, and brought misery upon it! See Ezra 9:1-2. Reader! remember what the Apostle saith, *Be ye not unequally yoked together with unbelievers; for what fellowship hath righteousness with unrighteousness? or what concord hath Christ with Belial?*[6]

What a sweet thought is that of the apostle: *The gifts and callings of God* (he saith) *are without repentance.*[7] Though it is said, God repented that he had *made* man; yet it is nowhere said, he repented that he *redeemed* him.

May it be my mercy, to remember, while reading the account of Noah's finding favor with God, that it is by him alone, of whom Noah was a type, even the Lord Jesus Christ, that I can find favor and acceptance

---

6   2 Corinthians 6:14.

7   Romans 11:29.

with God in this life, or salvation in another. In him, as the True Ark, may I be found, when God shall arise to judge the world. (Hawker, Poor Man's Old Testament Commentary: Genesis-Numbers, 30)

Day 7

Reading: Genesis 7

"... the Lord shut him in." Genesis 7:16

Noah was shut in away from all the world by the hand of divine love. The door of electing purpose interposes between us and the world which lieth in the wicked one. We are not of the world even as our Lord Jesus was not of the world. Into the sin, the gaiety, the pursuits of the multitude we cannot enter; we cannot play in the streets of Vanity Fair with the children of darkness, for our heavenly Father has shut us in. Noah was shut in *with his God.* "*Come* thou into the ark," was the Lord's invitation, by which he clearly showed that he himself intended to dwell in the ark with his servant and his family. Thus all the chosen dwell in God and God in them. Happy people to be enclosed in the same circle which contains God in the Trinity of his persons, Father, Son, and Spirit. Let us never be inattentive to that gracious call, "Come, my people, enter thou into thy chambers, and shut thy doors about thee, and hide thyself as it were for a little moment until the indignation be overpast." Noah was so shut in that *no evil could reach him.* Floods did but lift him heavenward, and winds did but waft him on his way. Outside of the ark all was ruin, but inside all was rest and peace. Without Christ we perish, but in Christ Jesus there is perfect safety. Noah was so shut in that he *could not even desire to come out*, and those who are in Christ Jesus are in him forever. They shall go no more out for ever, for eternal faithfulness has shut them in, and infernal malice cannot drag them out. The Prince of the house of David shutteth and no man openeth; and when once in the last days as Master of the house he shall rise up and shut the door, it will be in vain for mere professors to knock, and cry Lord, Lord open unto us, for that same door which shuts in the wise virgins will shut out the foolish forever. Lord, shut me in by thy grace. (Spurgeon, Morning, Jun 5)

Day 8

Reading: Genesis 8

"The dove came in to him in the evening." Genesis 8:11

Blessed be the Lord for another day of mercy, even though I am now weary with its toils. Unto the preserver of men lift I my song of gratitude. The dove found no rest out of the ark, and therefore returned to it; and my soul has learned yet more fully than ever, this day, that there is no satisfaction to be found in earthly things—God alone can give rest to my spirit. As to my business, my possessions, my family, my attainments, these are all well enough in their way, but they cannot fulfil the desires of my immortal nature. "Return unto thy rest, O my soul, for the Lord hath dealt bountifully with thee."[8] It was at the still hour, when the gates of the day were closing, that with weary wing the dove came back to the master: O Lord, enable me this evening thus to return to Jesus. She could not endure to spend a night hovering over the restless waste, not can I bear to be even for another hour away from Jesus, the rest of my heart, the home of my spirit. She did not merely alight upon the roof of the ark, she "came in to him;" even so would my longing spirit look into the secret of the Lord, pierce to the interior of truth, enter into that which is within the veil, and reach to my Beloved in very deed. To Jesus must I come: short

8   Psalm 116:7

of the nearest and dearest intercourse with him my panting spirit cannot stay. Blessed Lord Jesus, be with me, reveal thyself, and abide with me all night, so that when I awake I may be still with thee. I note that the dove brought in her mouth an olive branch plucked off, the memorial of the past day, and a prophecy of the future. Have I no pleasing record to bring home? No pledge and earnest of lovingkindness yet to come? Yes, my Lord, I present thee my grateful acknowledgments for tender mercies which have been new every morning and fresh every evening; and now, I pray thee, put forth thy hand and take thy dove into thy bosom. (Spurgeon, Eve, Jan 29)

Day 9

Reading: Genesis 9

"Whenever I form clouds over the earth and the bow appears in the clouds," Genesis 9:14

The rainbow, the symbol of the covenant with Noah, is typical of our Lord Jesus, who is the Lord's witness to the people. When may we *expect to see the token of the covenant?* The rainbow is only to be seen painted upon a *cloud.* When the sinner's conscience is dark with clouds, when he remembers his past sin, and mourneth and lamenteth before God, Jesus Christ is revealed to him as the covenant Rainbow, displaying all the glorious hues of the divine character and betokening peace. To the believer, when his trials and temptations surround him, it is sweet to behold the person of our Lord Jesus Christ—to see him bleeding, living, rising, and pleading for us. God's rainbow is hung over the cloud of our sins, our sorrows, and our woes, to prophesy deliverance. Nor does a *cloud* alone give a rainbow, there must be *the crystal drops* to reflect the light of the sun. So, our sorrows must not only threaten, but they must really fall upon us. There had been no Christ for us if the vengeance of God had been merely a threatening cloud: punishment must fall in terrible drops upon the Surety. Until there is a *real* anguish in the sinner's conscience, there is no Christ for him; until the chastisement which he feels becomes grievous, he cannot see Jesus. But there must also be a sun; for clouds and drops of rain make not rainbows unless the sun shineth. Beloved, our God, who is as the sun to us, always shines, but we do not always see him—clouds hide his face; but no matter what drops may be falling, or what clouds may be threatening, if *he* does but shine there will be a rainbow at once. It is said that when we see the rainbow the shower is over. Certain it is, that when Christ comes, our troubles remove; when we behold Jesus, our sins vanish, and our doubts and fears subside. When Jesus walks the waters of the sea, how profound the calm! (Spurgeon, Eve, Aug 12)

Day 10

Reading: Genesis 10

"... The nations on earth spread out from these after the flood." Genesis 10:32

This Chapter contains the history of the first branching out of the race of men, into families and households, of which, in after ages, the whole earth is overspread. Here are no less than seventy distinct roots of nations noticed, but only one nation upon earth, and that is, God's ancient people, the Jews, who can say from which of the seventy it sprung. The sacred historian gives a short account of the posterity of Japheth, and of Ham, but enlargeth chiefly upon that of Shem, because from that stock, after the flesh, the Messiah was to arise.

How graciously hath God watched over the promised seed, in the family of *Shem*, and so particularly marked down the descendants of the chosen race, from whom, after the flesh, that Holy Thing (as he is emphatically called in his own word) was to spring, Christ in the flesh, who is over all, God blessed forever. And how graciously hath God been pleased to note the features of his people in every age, by that uniform mark, by which they are known, of a poor and afflicted people. While the posterity of *Ham* are said to be the *Nimrods* of the earth; the offspring of *Shem*, with whom the blessing was deposited, is among the bond-slaves in Egypt. Let this teach us, how much better it is to be poor and humble, while belonging to the household of faith, than, void of faith, to be found related even to nobles. (Hawker, Poor Man's Old Testament Commentary: Genesis-Numbers, 42-43, 45)

Day 11

Reading: Genesis 11

"... the LORD confused the language of the whole earth ..." Genesis 11:9

What an awful view is here again afforded of man's apostacy! So little effect had the remembrance of the deluge left upon the human mind, that instead of being humbled under the mighty hand of God, we behold the workings of the heart occupied in contriving a plan to counteract the divine sovereignty in future. Perhaps infidelity, which is the same in all ages, ventured to do, what it is forever doing, to put down to *second* causes what was evidently the effect of a *first* ordination; and denied any divine interference in the flood of waters. Alas! my soul, what are all the rebellious murmurings and transgressions arising in my heart, but the effects of the same cause, unbelief! Lord I would pray, (as a pious father of old used to pray) "Preserve me from that evil man, myself."

I cannot close this chapter without stopping to remark, how striking an instance of the sovereignty of Almighty grace is here given, when we consider that from the confusion of languages, sent as a judgment in this instance, arose, in after ages, an occasion for the display of mercy, in the gift of tongues, to the Apostles; so that the wonders of the day of Pentecost sprung out of the ruins of *Babel*. What a precious testimony to the truth of that scripture: *Surely the wrath of man shall praise thee; the remainder of wrath shalt thou restrain.*[9] (Hawker, Poor Man's Old Testament Commentary: Genesis-Numbers, 49)

---

9   Psalm 76:10.

Day 12

Reading: Job 1

"... The Lord gives, and the Lord takes away. Blessed be the name of the Lord." Job 1:21

Bereaved Christian, God has smitten, and the stroke has fallen heavily. The blessing you thought you could the least spare, and would be the last to leave you, God your Father has taken. Why has He done this? To show you what He can be in your extremity. It may be difficult for faith, in the first moments of your calamity, to see how it can be well to be thus afflicted; but be still and wait the issue. Banish from your mind every hard thought of God, stifle in your breast every rebellious feeling, suppress upon your lip every repining word, and bow meekly, submissively, mutely, to the sovereign, righteous will of your Father. The blessings, like spring flowers blooming on the grave over which you weep, that will grow out of this affliction, will prove that God never loved you more deeply, was never more intent upon advancing your best interests, never thought more of you, nor cared more for you, than at the moment when His hand laid your loved one low. Receive the testimony of one who has tasted, ay, has drunk deeply, of the same cup of grief which your Father God now mingles for you. Let us drink it without a murmur. It is our Father's cup. As a father pities his children, so does He pity us even while He mingles and presents the draught. It is bitter, but not the bitterness of the curse; it is dark, but not the frown of anger; the cup is brimmed, but not a drop of wrath is there! Oh, wondrous faith that can look upon the beautiful stem broken; the lovely, promising flower, just unfolding its perfection, smitten; the toils and hopes of years, and in a moment, extinguished, and yet can say – "It is well!" Go, now, you precious treasure! God will have my heart, Christ would not I should be satisfied with His gift of love, but that I should be satisfied with His love without the gift. "You only are my portion, O Lord." The world looks dreary, life has lost a charm, the heart is smitten and withered like grass, some of its dearest earthly affections have gone down into the tomb, but He who recalled the blessing is greater and dearer than the blessing, and is Himself just the same as when He gave it. Jesus would be glorified by our resting in, and cleaving to, Him as our portion, even when the flowers of earthly beauty and the yet more precious fruits of spiritual comfort and consolation wither and depart. Satan would suggest that we have sinned away our blessings and forfeited our comforts, and that therefore the Lord is now hiding His face from us, and in anger shutting up His tender mercies. But this is not really so; He is hiding the flowers, but not Himself. In love to them, He is transferring them to His garden in heaven; and in love to us, He thus seeks to draw us nearer to His heart. He would have us knock at His door, and ask for a fresh cluster. We cherish our blessings, and rest in our comforts, and live upon our frames and feelings, and lose sight of and forget Him. He removes those who we might be always coming to Him for more. Oh, matchless love of Jesus!

But the place where the clearest view is taken of the present unfathomable dispensations of God, and where their unfolding light and unveiling glory wake the sweetest, loudest response to this truth – "He has done all things well" – is heaven. The glorified saint has closed his pilgrimage; life's dark shadows have melted into endless light; he now looks back upon the desert he traversed, upon the path he trod, and as in the full blaze of glory each page unfolds of his wondrous history, testifying to some new recorded instance of the lovingkindness and faithfulness of God, the grace, compassion, and sympathy of Jesus, the full heart exclaims – "He has done all things well." The past dealings of God with him in providence now appear most illustrious to the glorified mind. The machinery of Divine government, which here seemed so complex and inexplicable, now appears in all its harmony and beauty. Its mysteries are all unraveled, its problems are all solved, its events are all explained, and the promise of the Master has received its utmost fulfillment, "What I do you know not now but you shall know hereafter."[10] That dispensation that was enshrouded in such mystery; that event that flung so dark a shadow on the path; that affliction that seemed so conflicting with all our ideas of God's infinite wisdom, truth, and love; that stroke that crushed us to the earth – all now appears but parts of a perfect whole; and every providence in his past history, as it now passes in review, bathed in the liquid light of glory, swells the anthem – "HE HAS DONE ALL THINGS WELL!" (Winslow, Evening Thoughts, Oct 27)

---

10   John 13:7.

Day 13

Reading: Job 2

"They met together to go and sympathize with him and comfort him." Job 2:11

There is somewhat very interesting in this account. The uncommonly heavy afflictions of Job, had called forth, not only the pity and compassion of those men, but also their desires to the attempt of saying, or doing, what they could to alleviate his sorrows. It is a gospel precept, *to mourn with them that mourn.* And among gracious minds the Lord sometimes, and not unfrequently, affords a mutual holy joy in our visits of love, not only to those we go to comfort, but to ourselves also. It is a profitable service to visit gracious souls in their affliction, especially if we pray the Lord Jesus to go with us, and be of the party. *Better to go.* (saith Solomon) *to the house of mourning than the house of feasting.*[11] (Hawker, Poor Man's Old Testament Commentary: Job-Psalms, 12)

---

11   Ecclesiastes 7:2.

Day 14

Reading: Job 3

"After this, Job began to speak and cursed the day he was born." Job 3:1

It is worthy our closest observation in this account of Job, (and indeed it is one of the most important considerations in his history) that in the example of great and good men, the Holy Spirit hath been pleased to open to the view of the church, their frailties and imperfections also. While we are called upon to behold the patience of Job, James 5:11, we are to be taught, no less, that he was a man of like passions with ourselves. So in the examples of David, Peter, and others. Jeremiah acted as Job did under his affliction: Jeremiah 20:14–18. What Job hath said of the day of a man's birth, indeed, as it concerns our being born in sin, is true enough. And in this spiritual sense, the day of our death, when we die to sin, and are new born unto a life of righteousness in Jesus, by the quickening of the Spirit, is, as the wise man observes, far better. Ecclesiastes 7:1. But, otherwise, a child of God, under the heaviest affliction, hath a consolation in Jesus, to sweeten all. Reader! if the Lord, in infinite mercy, hath given you and me a new life, what blessings may we trace, both in our old creation, and in our new? Many a poor sinner hath been tempted to curse the day of his birth in nature. Oh! how may you and I bless the day of our new birth in grace! (Hawker, Poor Man's Old Testament Commentary: Job-Psalms, 14)

Day 15

Reading: Job 4

My soul! here are some very sweet instructions to be gathered from this chapter. In whatever light Eliphaz, the Temanite, be considered, still the Holy Spirit can and will make his conduct minister to the glory of God, and the good of God's children. His observations, in several parts, plainly teach God's people, whose remains of indwelling corruption are too apt to break out in murmuring under their afflictions, that there is no case, nor situation, in which a child of God can be placed, that for a moment can admit of dissatisfaction. But his observations no less teach at the same time, even in this point of view, that godly men make too light of God's afflictions, when they add to the smart, by giving unseasonable addition to the afflicted, in saying or doing whatever may serve to irritate and aggravate their sorrows. Certain it is, that Satan's grand artifice was to vex Job; so to conduct himself that, in the impulse of the moment, he might charge God foolishly, and curse him. And if the conversation of Eliphaz, however plausible, had a tendency to accomplish the same end, whatever the Temanite was in himself, he was evidently Satan's instrument to cast down the godly. Methinks I would therefore learn from hence, caution, even in a zeal for God and his glory, not to add to an heart that is vexed; but sweetly draw off the mind of any poor sufferer, which comes within my way, from brooding over the affliction, to look at the God of all our mercies in the affliction; or, to use the beautiful words of the prophet, to call upon the sufferer *to hear the rod, and who hath appointed it.*[12] And how should I do this so effectually, either in mine own sorrows, or the sorrows of others, as by looking to thee, thou blessed Jesus, in whose unequalled sorrows every child of God would soonest learn to forget his own. Oh! thou blessed Jesus! how doth thy bright example tend to dignify the path of suffering, and to give a luster to the tears of the heaviest affliction. Oh! for grace to follow thee by faith to the garden, to the wilderness, to the cross, and there meditate, until the soul goeth forth in the interesting enquiry, *Is it nothing to you, all ye that pass by: behold, and see if there be any sorrow like unto my sorrow which is done unto me, wherewith the Lord hath afflicted me in the day of his fierce anger?* (Hawker, Poor Man's Old Testament Commentary: Job-Psalms, 19–20)

---

12   Micah 6:9.

Day 16

Reading: Job 5

"I would appeal to God and would present my case to him. He does great and unsearchable things, wonders without number." Job 5:8-9

The best improvement that we can make under God the Holy Spirit, from this discourse of the man of *Timan*, is to consider the whole scope of his reasoning, not as it concerns Job only, but all the exercised family of the faithful upon earth. As far as we have already advanced, in the history of this patriarch's sufferings, we trace enough to discover some of the sweet designs of the Lord in his affliction! God will manifest that Satan's charge is false. Job's integrity shall be proved. And therefore, Job's integrity must be brought to the trial. The enemy charged him with hypocrisy. And Job's friends are endeavoring to prove it, During the sharp exercise the Lord will sustain him.

Reader! remark from what we have already seen in Job's history, that a suitableness of mind and heart under trial, is one of the highest attainments of faith. There is little or no exercise for faith, when all things go well. When the Lord in his providence, neither suffers our desires to be crossed, nor thwarts our wishes; then it is smooth sailing down the stream of life. But if God raiseth a storm; permits the enemy to send wave after wave, and when we cry the Lord gives no answer, but seemingly stands aloof from our prayers; then in the prospect of shipwreck, still to hang on and trust God, when we cannot trace him; this is the patience of the saints!

But oh! precious Jesus, how sweet is it to eye thee, thou blessed Author and Finisher of faith in such moments. While we look at thee what strength doth it induce! when we lose sight of thee, what poor creatures the best of thy servants are! Oh! Lord! I would say for myself and Reader, give us to believe! help thou our unbelief. (Hawker, Poor Man's Old Testament Commentary: Job-Psalms, 23–24)

Day 17

Reading: Job 6

"If only my grief could be weighed and my devastation placed with it on the scales." Job 6:2

There is a great beauty here manifesting itself, in the wish of Job for a Mediator; for I hope the Reader will not overlook what is plainly implied, in all these several expressions. Job tells Eliphaz and his friends with him, that their incompetency of knowing what his grief was, made both him and them, think lighter of it than it really was. Therefore, saith Job, Oh! that it were weighed! Are not these the cries both of nature and grace, after one that could weigh them? Job perfectly knew that the Almighty, whose arrows he says were within him, could not be ignorant of the depth of his sorrows. But if there was a day's man, a mediator, who from a perfect knowledge of his state, could graciously stand up between God and his soul, to plead his cause and make his peace: this would be the desire of his heart. Reader! how sweet is it to remark, the universal voice of every enlightened mind, from the first transgressor in the garden of Eden, to the coming of the promised seed, all sending forth their most fervent cries, for this glorious, gracious Mediator! Did not Adam say as much when he cried out, I heard thy voice in the garden, and I was afraid?[13] And did not Israel do the same, when they cried unto Moses; go thou near and hear all that

13   Genesis 3:10.

the Lord our God shall say, and speak thou unto us, all that the Lord our God shall speak?[14] What are these instances, with many others that might be brought forward in proof, but testimonies, that it is a Mediator, the soul oppressed with sin and sorrow, hath been longing for in all ages. Reader! think of your happiness in having one, so sweetly revealed to you, and one so near to you, and so near to God? (Hawker, Poor Man's Old Testament Commentary: Job-Psalms, 24-25)

---

14   Deuteronomy 5:27.

Day 18

Reading: Job 7

"Am I the sea, or a sea monster, that you keep me under guard?" Job 7:12

This was a strange question for Job to ask of the Lord. He felt himself to be too insignificant to be so strictly watched and chastened, and he hoped that he was not so unruly as to need to be so restrained. The enquiry was natural from one surrounded with such insupportable miseries, but after all, it is capable of a very humbling answer. It is true man is not the sea, but he is even more troublesome and unruly. The sea obediently respects its boundary, and though it be but a belt of sand, it does not overleap the limit. Mighty as it is, it hears the divine *hitherto*, and when most raging with tempest it respects the word; but self-willed man defies heaven and oppresses earth, neither is there any end to this rebellious rage. The sea, obedient to the moon, ebbs and flows with ceaseless regularity, and thus renders an active as well as a passive obedience; but man, restless beyond his sphere, sleeps within the lines of duty, indolent where he should be active. He will neither come nor go at the divine command, but sullenly prefers to do what he should not, and to leave undone that which is required of him. Every drop in the ocean, every beaded bubble, and every yeasty foam-flake, every shell and pebble, feel the power of law, and yield or move at once. O that our nature were but one thousandth part as much conformed to the will of God! We call the sea fickle and false, but how constant it is! Since our fathers' days, and the old time before them, the sea is where it was, beating on the same cliffs to the same tune; we know where to find it, it forsakes not its bed, and changes not in its ceaseless boom; but where is man-vain, fickle man? Can the wise man guess by what folly he will next be seduced from his obedience? We need more watching than the billowy sea, and are far more rebellious. Lord, rule us for thine own glory. Amen. (Spurgeon, Eve, Sep 16)

Day 19

Reading: Job 8

"Can the rush grow up without mire?" Job 8:11 (AKJV)

The rush is spongy and hollow, and even so is a hypocrite; there is no substance or stability in him. It is shaken to and fro in every wind just as formalists yield to every influence; for this reason, the rush is not broken by the tempest, neither are hypocrites troubled with persecution. I would not willingly be a deceiver or be deceived; perhaps the text for this day may help me to try myself whether I be a hypocrite or no. The rush by nature lives in water, and owes its very existence to the mire and moisture wherein it has taken root; let the mire become dry, and the rush withers very quickly. Its greenness is absolutely dependent upon circumstances, a present abundance of water makes it flourish, and a drought destroys it at once. Is this my case? Do I only serve God when I am in good company, or when religion is profitable and respectable? Do I love the Lord only when temporal comforts are received from his hands? If so I am a base hypocrite, and like the withering rush, I shall perish when death deprives me of outward joys. But can I honestly assert that when bodily comforts have been few, and my surroundings have been rather adverse to grace than at all helpful to it, I have still held fast my integrity? then have

I hope that there is genuine vital godliness in me. The rush cannot grow without mire, but plants of the Lord's right-hand planting can and do flourish even in the year of drought. A godly man often grows best when his worldly circumstances decay. He who follows Christ for his bag is a Judas; they who follow for loaves and fishes are children of the devil; but they who attend him out of love to himself are his own beloved ones. Lord, let me find my life in thee, and not in the mire of this world's favor or gain. (Spurgeon, Morning, Dec 27)

Day 20

Reading: Job 9

"If he passed by me, I wouldn't see him; if he went by, I wouldn't recognize him. If he snatches something, who can stop him? Who can ask him, "What are you doing?"" Job 9:11-12

And is this the way of the Lord with you, my beloved? Are you bewildered at the mazes through which you are threading your steps; at the involved circumstances of your present history? Deem yourself not alone in this. No mystery has lighted upon your path but what is common to the one family of God: "This honor have all his saints." The Shepherd is leading you, as all the flock is led, with a skillful hand, and in a right way. It is yours to stand if He bids you, or to follow if He leads. "He gives no account of any of His matters," assuming that His children have such confidence in His wisdom, and love, and uprightness, as in all the wonder-working of His dealings with them, to "be still and know that He is God."[15] Throw back a glance upon the past, and see how little you have ever understood of all the way God has led you. What a mystery – perhaps now better explained – has enveloped His whole proceedings! When Joseph, for example, was torn from the homestead of his father, sold, and borne a slave into Egypt, not a syllable of that eventful page of his history could he spell. And yet God's way with

15   Psalm 46:10.

this His servant was perfect. And could Joseph have seen at the moment that he descended into the pit, where he was cast by his envious brethren, all the future of his history as vividly and as palpably as be beheld it in after years, while there would have been the conviction that all was well, we doubt not that faith would have lost much of its vigor, and God much of His glory.[16] And so, with good old Jacob. The famine, the parting with Benjamin, the menacing conduct of Pharaoh's prime minister, wrung the mournful expression from his lips, "All these things are against me."[17] All was veiled in deep and mournful mystery. Thus, was it with Job, to whom God spoke from the whirlwind that swept every vestige of affluence and domestic comfort from his dwelling. And thus, too, with Naomi, when she exclaimed, "Call me not Naomi, call me Mara: for the Almighty has dealt very bitterly with me. I went out full, and the Lord has brought me home again empty."[18] That it is to the honor of God to conceal, should in our view justify all His painful and humiliating procedure with us. "It is the glory of God to conceal a thing," as it will be for His endless glory, by and by, fully to reveal it all. But there is one thing, Christian sufferer, which He cannot conceal. He cannot conceal the love that forms the spring and foundation of all His conduct with His saints. Do what He will, conceal as He may, be His chariot the thick clouds, and His way in the deep sea, still His love betrays itself, disguised though it may be in dark and impenetrable providence. There are under-

---

16   Genesis 37-50.

17   Genesis 42:36.

18   Ruth 1:20-21.

tones, gentle and tender, in the roughest accents of our Joseph's voice. And he who has an ear ever hearkening to the Lord shall often exclaim, "Speak, Lord, how and when and where you may – it is the voice of my Beloved!" (Winslow, Evening Thoughts, Jan 6)

Day 21

Reading: Job 10

"... Let me know why you prosecute me." Job 10:2

Perhaps, O tried soul, the Lord is doing this to develop thy graces. There are some of thy graces which would never be *discovered* if it were not for thy trials. Dost thou not know that thy faith never looks so grand in summer weather as it does in winter? Love is too often like a glow-worm, showing but little light except it be in the midst of surrounding darkness. Hope itself is like a star—not to be seen in the sunshine of prosperity, and only to be discovered in the night of adversity. Afflictions are often the black foils in which God doth set the jewels of his children's graces, to make them shine the better. It was but a little while ago that on thy knees thou wast saying, "Lord, I fear I have no faith: let me know that I have faith." Was not this really, though perhaps unconsciously, praying for trials? – for how canst thou know that thou hast faith until thy faith is exercised? Depend upon it, God often sends us trials that our graces may be discovered, and that we may be certified of their existence. Besides, it is not merely discovery, *real growth* in grace is the result of sanctified trials. God often takes away our comforts and our privileges in order to make us better Christians. He trains his soldiers, not in tents of ease and luxury, but by turning them out and using them to forced marches and hard service. He makes them ford through streams, and swim through rivers, and climb mountains, and walk many a long mile with heavy knapsacks of sorrow on their backs. Well, Christian, may not this account for the troubles through which thou art passing? Is not the Lord bringing out your graces, and making them grow? Is not this the reason why he is contending with you?

"Trials make the promise sweet;

Trials give new life to prayer;

Trials bring me to his feet,

Lay me low, and keep me there."

(Spurgeon, Morning, Feb 18)

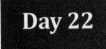

Reading: Job 11

Reader! how happy is it for you and for me, that we live under a brighter dispensation, than Job's counsellors, and are taught by him in whom are hid all the treasures of wisdom and knowledge. Yes! blessed Jesus! thou hast taught that great afflictions not only may abound among those whom God loveth, but that heavy trials and temptations, when found in the path of godliness, are rather testimonies of vine favor. Thou hast said thyself; *As many as I love, I rebuke and chasten.*[19] I beseech thee, therefore, blessed Master, that I may eye thee in every dispensation, and then sure I am, that I shall discover love at the bottom of all thine appointments, and wisdom guiding and regulating all. My Jesus, while he governs as my God, will never forget that he is also my Savior, my brother, my husband, my friend. And if such views as these, will not stop the voice of complaint, nothing will. And dearest, blessed Master, while I thus beseech thee to grant me grace and strength equal to my day, that I may be always on the lookout for thy wise and loving government in all things: yet when it shall please thee, as most suited to thy good will and pleasure, to hide from me thy plan, and as with Job, things are mysterious, and discouraging; yet even then, blessed Lord, never, oh never, remit the communications of thy grace within,

---

19   Revelation 3:19.

that faith may be in lively exercise, and that I may find strength from thee, to trust thee when I cannot trace thee. Let the storm from without beat ever so violently, yet if my Jesus support the roof within, my poor frail tabernacle will not fall. Oh! for the sweet consolations and lovely teachings of Jesus, by his Spirit, that I may be able to say, at the worst of times, I see enough of Jesus in this dispensation, to be assured it is in his appointment! It must therefore be among the all things which work together for good. It shall be well. I shall wade through this affliction, as I have, by the Lord's leading me, through many before. Here then, blessed Lord, I will rest. Though I see thee not in all these providences of thine, it is enough that thou seest me? and art not only looking on, but tempering my trials to my strength, and hast promised to stay thy rough wind in the day of thy east wind. Though, like the disciples, my soul may fear as I enter the cloud, yet Jesus will be there, and he will shine out, and shine through all. By and by, every intervening cloud will be forever taken out of the way; and he that is now my God and my salvation, will be my everlasting light, my God, and my glory. (Hawker, Poor Man's Old Testament Commentary: Job-Psalms, 44-45)

Reading: Job 12

"Wisdom and strength belong to God; counsel and understanding are his." Job 12:13

Reader! you and I shall go over this sweet and interesting book of Job to very little good, if we do not, as we read it, look up for the teaching of the Holy Spirit, and seek from it to search our own interest in what we meet with in the several chapters. Our own life is the most important of all lives to be well versed in: and depend upon it, what we meet with in the history of Job and his friends, may, in numberless occasions, under the Spirit's teaching, be made profitable to our own. It was a blessed command the man of God had in commission to give the church, when he said, 'Thou shalt remember all the way which the Lord thy God led thee these forty years in the wilderness, to humble thee, and to prove thee, to know what was in thine heart, whether thou wouldest keep his commandments, or no.'[20] Under this idea, is there nothing in what we have already reviewed of Job's history, applicable to ourselves? Is not Satan accusing us as he did Job? Hath our gracious God permitted him to harass us with his devices? Have we the unkindness of friends, or the malice of open enemies, to grapple with also? Hath the Lord brought us under any bereaving providences; any bodily or <u>spiritual</u> afflictions? How are we exercised on any

20   Deuteronomy 8:2.

of these occasions! Pause, Reader! look into your own heart, as I pray God to search mine. How are we dealing with God; and how is the Lord dealing with us? Oh! Sir, depend upon it, that is ever a sweet mercy, however harsh it may at first seem, which, in the close, brings the soul to Jesus. The medicine we take may be nauseous, but its, effect is salutary. Job was stripped of all his earthly comforts but Job lost not his God. This brought him up. Let our bodies be ever so poor, ever so sickly, ever so sore, yet, if we have Jesus formed in our souls, the hope of glory, here is enough to sing Hallelujah in the whole. And if the trials the Lord sends come with a commission to lead to Jesus, surely love was at the bottom, and by and by our praises will be called forth in acknowledgment. Lord, I would say for myself and Reader, give us both grace to be ever on the look-out for the Lord's manifestations to us, and our proper and wise use of them; and then we shall assuredly find that *at evening time it will be light.*[21] Mercy and goodness have been following us all the days of our life, until we come to dwell in the house of our God for ever. (Hawker, Poor Man's Old Testament Commentary: Job-Psalms, 48)

21   Zechariah 14:7.

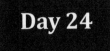

Reading: Job 13

"How many iniquities and sins have I committed?"
Job 13:23

Have you ever really weighed and considered how great the sin of God's people is? Think how heinous is your own transgression, and you will find that not only does a sin here and there tower up like an alp, but that your iniquities are heaped upon each other, as in the old fable of the giants who piled Pelian upon Ossa, mountain upon mountain. What an aggregate of sin there is in the life of one of the most sanctified of God's children! Attempt to multiply this, the sin of one only, by the multitude of the redeemed, "a number which no man can number," and you will have some conception of the great mass of the guilt of the people for whom Jesus shed his blood. But we arrive at a more adequate idea of the magnitude of sin by the greatness of the remedy provided. It is the blood of Jesus Christ, God's only and well-beloved Son. God's Son! Angels cast their crowns before him! All the choral symphonies of heaven surround his glorious throne. "God over all, blessed forever. Amen." And yet he takes upon himself the form of a servant, and is scourged and pierced, bruised and torn, and at last slain; since nothing but the blood of the incarnate Son of God could make atonement for our offences. No human mind can adequately estimate

the infinite value of the divine sacrifice, for great
as is the sin of God's people, the atonement which
takes it away is immeasurably greater. Therefore, the
believer, even when sin rolls like a black flood, and
the remembrance of the past is bitter, can yet stand
before the blazing throne of the great and holy God,
and cry, "Who is he that condemneth? It is Christ
that died; yea rather, that hath risen again."[22] While
the recollection of his sin fills him with shame and
sorrow, he at the same time makes it a foil to show
the brightness of mercy—guilt is the dark night in
which the fair star of divine love shines with serene
splendor. (Spurgeon, Eve, Jul 6)

---

22   Romans 8:34.

Reading: Job 14

"... I would wait all the days of my struggle until my relief comes." Job 14:14

A little stay on earth will make heaven more heavenly. Nothing makes rest so sweet as toil; nothing renders security so pleasant as exposure to alarms. The bitter quassia cups of earth will give a relish to the new wine which sparkles in the golden bowls of glory. Our battered armor and scarred countenances will render more illustrious our victory above, when we are welcomed to the seats of those who have overcome the world. We should not have full *fellowship with Christ* if we did not for a while sojourn below, for he was baptized with a baptism of suffering among men, and we must be baptized with the same if we would share his kingdom. Fellowship with Christ is so honorable that the sorest sorrow is a light price by which to procure it. Another reason for our lingering here is *for the good of others*. We would not wish to enter heaven till our work is done, and it may be that we are yet ordained to minister light to souls benighted in the wilderness of sin. Our prolonged stay here is doubtless *for God's glory*. A tried saint, like a well-cut diamond, glitters much in the King's crown. Nothing reflects so much honor on a workman as a protracted and severe trial of his work, and its triumphant endurance of the ordeal without giving way in any part. We are God's workmanship, in whom he will be glorified by our afflictions. It is for the honor of Jesus that we endure the trial of our faith with sacred joy. Let each man surrender his own longings to the glory of Jesus, and feel, "If my lying in the dust would elevate my Lord by so much as an inch, let me still lie among the pots of earth. If to live on earth forever would make my Lord more glorious, it should be my heaven to be shut out of heaven." Our time is fixed and settled by eternal decree. Let us not be anxious about it, but wait with patience till the gates of pearl shall open. (Spurgeon, Eve, May 6)

Day 26

Reading: Job 15

"What is a mere human, that he should be pure, or one born of a woman, that he should be righteous?" Job 15:14

R eader! let us pause over what we have been reading of the aggravated afflictions of Job. Was it not enough that the Lord was exercising his servant, but those three men must throw in their unkind and unjust interpretations of God's dealings? Surely those sharp and bitter reproaches could not fail to add to poor Job's misery. We naturally look round in our sorrows for some to commiserate. But this distressed sufferer, instead of consolation, met with nothing but reproof.

But let us pass over the view of men, that are but instruments, and behold how the Lord produces good from evil. Though no chastening for the present seemeth to be joyous, but grievous, nevertheless, afterward it yieldeth the peaceable fruits of righteousness to them that are exercised thereby. No calamity, no stroke of trouble, however heavy, however severe, can rob a follower of the Lord of his favor. Nothing can take away our Christ, that first, and best, and comprehensive gift of a covenant God! *What shall separate us from the love of Christ?* (saith Paul) *Neither death, nor life,* (saith the apostle) *neither things present, nor things to come.*[23] Having him then, in him we possess all things.

But, Reader! let us not close this chapter of the relation of Job's sufferings, nor indeed any other, without looking beyond Job, to him that was the Prince of Sufferers, as he was the Prince of Peace. Yes! blessed Jesus! it behooved thee, that in all things thou mightest have the pre-eminency. Oh! thou gracious Redeemer! how do all sorrows sink to nothing, when we behold thee in the garden, and on the tree; when we behold thy agony and bloody sweat, thy cross and passion; and hear that heart-piercing cry, *My God, my God, why hast thou forsaken me?*[24] And all this, not for thyself, but for thy people; not that thy holy life needed ought, but for thy voluntary grace and favor to our poor, lost, ruined, and undone nature: thou didst suffer, the just for the unjust, to bring us to God; and didst even admit the being deserted of thy Father for a space, that we might not be deserted forever! Boundless love of a most precious, loving Savior! (Hawker, Poor Man's Old Testament Commentary: Job-Psalms, 58-59)

---

23   Romans 8:35-39.
24   Matthew 27:46.

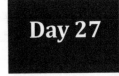

Reading: Job 16

"I wish that someone might argue for a man with God just as anyone would for a friend." Job 16:21

Perhaps in no part of Job's complaints doth the torrent with which his whole frame was overwhelmed rise higher, than in what is contained in this discourse (Job 16:7-18). His heart seemed to have been full, and he gives it vent. How exercised in his family, in his person, by the enemy of souls, the unkind and unjust reproaches of his friends; and to sum up all, his God looking on, and yet to his earnest cries returning no answer. Job knew not the blessed issue which awaited the whole, and therefore only spoke while under the full pressure of the accumulated burthens. There is a great elegance in the figure of Job's leanness, when he considered the wrinkles of his wasted body, as carrying about with him an unceasing witness to his grief. And the close of the complaint, in crying to the earth to cover not his blood, but to be above the ground in testimony for him; these are most striking expressions of the mind of Job.

But the greatest beauty of Job's discourse, and what I would above every other call upon the Reader to remark with me is, the earnest longing contained in the close of his address, in which he is so passionately looking out for the Mediator. Let the Reader look over again and again what Job here saith, *oh that one might plead for a man with God!* Then let him see that prayer answered, in the appointment of Jesus, as our Great High Priest and Intercessor; and then let him determine for himself, (for to his own heart under the blessed Spirit's teaching, I leave the subject for decision), whether Job had not an eye to Jesus; who is not only our Advocate with the Father, but is such in the very way which Job desired, even as the man Christ Jesus pleading for his neighbor, his poor brethren, his kinsmen after the flesh, and whom he is not ashamed to call brethren. Hebrews 2:11. (Hawker, Poor Man's Old Testament Commentary: Job-Psalms, 60-61)

Reading: Job 17

"My spirit is broken. My days are extinguished. A graveyard awaits me." Job 17:1

Reader! let you and I seek grace from the Lord, that we may gather from this chapter all the blessed improvements the Holy Spirit intended from it, to convey to his church and people. For you and I may with equal justness, take up Job's language as he did, and say, our breath is corrupt, our days are extinct, and the grave is ready for us. Whether Job's afflictions, or Job's trials, may be or not our portion in going home through our pilgrimage state, we know not. These things are in a wiser and better appointment than our own. But whether or not a time of trouble come, death *must* come; *for it is appointed unto all men once to die, and after this the judgment.*[25] And what an awful thing must it be, to be unprepared for what is so sure! Depend upon it, the man that lives at an uncertainty, will die at an uncertainty. How much doth the, example of Job recommend itself to our notice and imitation; if like him, we were to deal familiarly with death; take a turn often to the grave, and fancy ourselves as there, before that in reality we are carried there; this would tend to lessen the apprehension, and lead the soul into a serious enquiry, of the surest means of making it a peaceable and happy dwelling place. This would

25   Hebrews 9:27.

be to use the world as not abusing it, and to induce, under divine teaching, those blessed effects, which while prompting the heart to say to corruption, thou art my father; and to the worm, thou art my mother and my sister, would lead out the whole soul in desires after him, who by his death hath overcome death, and by his resurrection, hath secured the everlasting happiness of his redeemed. Yes! thou Great, thou Almighty Conqueror of death, hell, and the grave! This would be to become savingly acquainted with thee, and thy precious salvation, that both in a living hour, and in a dying hour, our hearts might be on the lookout for the Master's call, that whether it should be at midnight or at cockcrowing, or in the morning, we might be found like those wise servants, who wait for their Lord's approach. Precious Jesus! write thy gracious warning upon each heart, and grant us grace, to live up to the constant exercise of it, by faith in thy blood and righteousness: *Be ye always ready, for ye know not at what hour the Son of man cometh.*[26] (Hawker, Poor Man's Old Testament Commentary: Job-Psalms, 64–65)

---

26   Matthew 24:44.

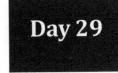

Reading: Job 18

"Indeed, such is the dwelling of the unjust man, and this is the place of the one who does not know God." Job 18:21

Our reflections on this chapter will be rendered profitable, if so be the Holy Spirit graciously make them so for us, in leading our minds to consider how very consistent it is, with the love the Lord hath to the persons of his people, as in the instance of Job, to chasten them for their departures and infirmities. Reader! only pause and consider how great, how dear, how inexpressibly costly our redemption was to God. And therefore, how suitable it is, that there should not be the smallest abuse of his covenant mercy, by his dear Son. Though Job was no hypocrite, yet Job confessed himself to be a sinner, sprung from the common stock of whom it is with truth said, there is none righteous, no not one. And there is in the best of men, even the most faithful servants of the Lord Jesus, so much of that commonness of corruption, belonging to a fallen nature, that if God's grace did not restrain it, the worst of sins would be the sad and deadly consequence breaking out in all. How blessed is it then to see in God's chastisement of our sin, though accepting the person of his people in Jesus, he manifests the holiness of his nature, and secures his own glory. And here, blessed Jesus, cause both

Writer and Reader to pause, and contemplate the unparalleled instance of this regard Jehovah had to his holiness, and to his glory, when for sin in us he put thee to grief. Never, surely, was there such a proof ever given. And never can there be any more the like to it; as when he made thee to be sin for us, though thou knewest no sin, that we might be made the righteousness of God in thee. Hail! thou holy, blessed, spotless Lamb of God. Oh! what unknown, what unnumbered, what never to be fully accounted for, or fully recompensed riches, blessings, glories, are contained in the one offering of thyself once for all, by which thou hast forever perfected them that are sanctified. Oh! write this precious thought upon my inmost soul, and let death itself never, never be able to blunt the remembrance of it; Jesus and his glorious redemption hath more to plead for his church before God and his Father, than all the church's sins can plead against them. Neither can eternity itself recompense the infinite merit of the righteousness and blood-shedding sacrifice of a God incarnate. (Hawker, Poor Man's Old Testament Commentary: Job-Psalms, 67)

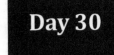

Day 30

Reading: Job 19

"I know that my Redeemer lives." Job 19:25

The marrow of Job's comfort lies in that little word "My" – "My Redeemer," and in the fact that the Redeemer lives. Oh! to get hold of a living Christ. We must get a property in him before we can enjoy him. What is gold in the mine to me? Men are beggars in Peru, and beg their bread in California. It is gold in my purse which will satisfy my necessities, by purchasing the bread I need. So, a Redeemer who does not redeem me, an avenger who will never stand up for my blood, of what avail were such? Rest not content until by faith you can say "Yes, I cast myself upon my living Lord; and he is mine." It may be you hold him with a feeble hand; you half think it presumption to say, "He lives as *my* Redeemer;" yet, remember if you have but faith as a grain of mustard seed, that little faith entitles you to say it. But there is also another word here, expressive of Job's strong confidence, *"I know."* To say, "I hope so, I trust so" is comfortable; and there are thousands in the fold of Jesus who hardly ever get much further. But to reach the essence of consolation you must say, "I know." Ifs, buts, and perhaps, are sure murderers of peace and comfort. Doubts are dreary things in times of sorrow. Like wasps they sting the soul! If I have any suspicion that Christ is not mine, then there is vinegar mingled with the gall of death; but if I know that Jesus lives for me, then darkness is not dark: even the night is light about me. Surely if Job, in those ages before the coming and advent of Christ, could say, "I know," *we* should not speak less positively. God forbid that our positiveness should be presumption. Let us see that our evidences are right, lest we build upon an ungrounded hope; and then let us not be satisfied with the mere foundation, for it is from the upper rooms that we get the widest prospect. A living Redeemer, truly mine, is joy unspeakable. (Spurgeon, Morning, Apr 21)

Day 31

Reading: Job 20

I have not interrupted the perusal of the whole discourse of Zophar's (Job 20:4-29), for there is no break in it from beginning to end. The observations arising out of it, therefore, are general observations, which may as well be taken in one point of view as separately. The chief scope of his preaching is, to shew the misery of the wicked, and the prosperity of the righteous. And if Zophar had connected the subject as referring to this life and another, and then insisted upon it that wickedness, must sooner or later, produce misery, all would have been well. But by confining his observations to the limits of this life only, and going upon that ground, that God never did, nor ever would afflict the righteous, he miserably mistakes the truths of God, and the universal experience of the faithful in all ages. Had he read the history of the Patriarchs, the cruel treatment of Joseph; the bondage of Israel in Egypt, and the like, he would have found the fallacy of his arguments; or had he known, what we know, of Jesus and his sorrows. And the Reader will take notice I hope, that to this ignorance, must be ascribed all the ill reasoning of all the discourses of Job's three friends. If we keep this therefore in view as we read their sermons, then we shall learn how to make the suitable improvements from them, and under this restriction, we shall find many striking observations, well deserving our notice and regard.

How beautifully doth Zophar describe, the wretched state of even the most prosperous sinner. How short are his triumphs; how fleeting and unsubstantial all his joy. Though he maketh his nest on high, and his head reacheth the clouds, yet this is only to make his fall more grievous and heavy. His name, his dwelling place, his memory, how soon forgotten. His sins lie down with him in the grave. His conscience, his thoughts, his whole heart always in alarm. What a finished representation of misery, doth Zophar give of the miserable state of wicked men while they live, and of the terrors in which they often die. But as the discourse of Zophar was directed personally to Job in all this, how unkind and unjust was the whole of his reasonings. How much sweeter is that short, but decisive passage of God by the prophet; *Say ye to the righteous that it shall be well with him; for they shall eat the fruit of their doings. Woe unto the wicked it shall be ill with him, for the reward of his hands shall be given him.*[27] (Hawker, Poor Man's Old Testament Commentary: Job-Psalms, 74-75)

---

27   Isaiah 3:10-11.

Reading: Job 21

Job gives, in [verses 8-13], a most masterly description of prosperous sinners: and every age of the Church affords numberless living examples, that the account is not heightened. Observe, what a view the man of Uz gives, in the first place, of their mirth. They are unvisited by affliction. The rod of God, as a kind father, is not felt by them. Observe the training of their children. What a melancholy picture is this of an ungodly house: They send them forth to the dance. Alas! what thousands of graceless parents there are, in the present day, who do this, and are regardless of their children's eternal welfare. They take the timbrel and the harp (the same fashionable instruments which the frivolous make a chief part of the education of our day); but not a word of taking the Bible, or the sweet sounds of the gospel of Jesus, for their little ones to be brought up in the knowledge of it: but the whole system tends to this end, how to excel in that, which the stage dancers and the lowest of animals excel in, as well as they! Observe in what striking terms Job describes the result of all this: *they spend their days in wealth, and in a moment go down to the grave.* And who that looks round, and contemplates what is daily going on in the carnal world before their eyes, can require further evidence of the truth of this now, as well as in Job's days. Read what Asaph hath remarked to the same effect, and compare the scriptures together, Psalm 73:3–20. (Hawker, Poor Man's Old Testament Commentary: Job-Psalms, 77)

Reading: Job 22

"Acquaint now thyself with him ..." Job 22:21

If we would rightly "acquaint ourselves with God, and be at peace," we must know him as he has revealed himself, not only in *the unity of his essence and subsistence*, but also in the *plurality of his persons.* God said, "Let us make man in our own image"[28]—let not man be content until he knows something of the "us" from whom his being was derived. Endeavour to know the Father; bury your head in his bosom in deep repentance, and confess that you are not worthy to be called his son; receive the kiss of his love; let the ring which is the token of his eternal faithfulness be on your finger; sit at his table and let your heart make merry in his grace. Then press forward and seek to know much of *the Son* of God who is the brightness of his Father's glory, and yet in unspeakable condescension of grace became man for our sakes; know him in the singular complexity of his nature: eternal God, and yet suffering, finite man; follow him as he walks the waters with the tread of deity, and as he sits upon the well in the weariness of humanity. Be not satisfied unless you know much of Jesus Christ as your Friend, your Brother, your Husband, your all. Forget not *the Holy Spirit*; endeavor to obtain a clear view of his nature and character, his attributes, and his works. Behold that Spirit of the

28   Genesis 1:26.

Lord, who first of all moved upon chaos, and brought forth order; who now visits the chaos of your soul, and creates the order of holiness. Behold him as the Lord and giver of spiritual life, the Illuminator, the Instructor, the Comforter, and the Sanctifier. Behold him as, like holy unction, he descends upon the head of Jesus, and then afterwards rests upon *you* who are as the skirts of his garments. Such an intelligent, scriptural, and experimental belief in the Trinity in Unity is yours if you truly know God; and such knowledge *brings peace indeed.* (Spurgeon, Eve, May 8)

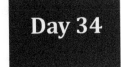

Reading: Job 23

" Yet he knows the way I have taken;" Job 23:10

Untried, untrodden, and unknown as your future path may be, it is, each step, mapped, arranged, and provided for in the everlasting and unchangeable covenant of God. To Him who leads us, who accepts us in the Son of His love, who knows the end from the beginning, it is no new, or uncertain, or hidden way. We thank Him that while He wisely and kindly veils all the future from our reach, all that future – its minutest event – is as transparent and visible to Him as the past. Our Shepherd knows the windings along which He skillfully, gently, and safely leads His flock. He has traveled that way Himself, and has left the traces of His presence on the road. And as each follower advances – the new path unfolding at each step – he can exultingly exclaim, "I see the footprint of my Lord; here went my Master, my Leader, my Captain, leaving me an example that I should follow His steps." Oh, it is a thought replete with strong consolation, and well calculated to gird us for the coming year – the Lord knows and has ordained each step of the untrodden path upon which I am about to enter.

Another reflection. The infinite forethought, wisdom, and goodness which have marked each line of our new path, have also provided for its every necessity. Each exigency in the history of the new year has been anticipated. Each need will bring its appropriate and adequate supply – each perplexity will have its guidance – each sorrow its comfort – each temptation its shield – each cloud its light. Each affliction will suggest its lesson – each correction will impart its teaching – each mercy will convey its message of love. The promise will be fulfilled to the letter, "As your day, so shall your strength be." (Winslow, Morning Thoughts, Jan 2)

Reading: Job 24

"The wicked are those who rebel against the light ..." Job 24:13a

So far from cooperating with the Spirit in the new creation, the natural man presents every resistance and opposition to it. There is not only a passive aversion to, but there is an active resistance of, the work. The stream of man's natural inclinations runs counter to all holiness. A strong and steady current has set in against God and all that God loves. The pride of reason, the perverseness of the will, the enmity of the mind, the heart's love of sin, all are up in arms against the entrance of the Holy Spirit. Satan, the great enemy of God and man, has been too long in quiet and undisturbed possession of the soul, to resign his dominion without a strong and a fearful struggle to maintain it. When the Spirit of God knocks at the door of the heart, every ally is summoned by the "strong man armed" to "quench the Spirit," and bar and bolt each avenue to his entrance. All is alarm, agitation, and commotion within. There is a danger of being dispossessed, and every argument, persuasion, and contrivance must be resorted to, in order to retain the long-undisputed throne. The world is summoned to throw out its most enticing bait – ambition, wealth, literary and political distinction, pleasure in her thousand forms of fascination and power – all are made to pass, as in review, before the mind. The flesh, exerts its influence – the love of sin is appealed to, affection for some long-cherished lust, some long-indulged habit, some "fond amusement," some darling taste – these, inspired with new vigor, are summoned to the rescue. Thus Satan, the world, and the flesh are opposed to the Father, the Son, and the Spirit, in the great work of spiritual regeneration. Oh, let no individual be so deceived as to believe, that when God the Eternal Spirit enters the soul, He finds the temple swept, and garnished, and prepared for His reception – that without the exercise of His own omnipotent and irresistible power, the heart bounds to welcome Him, the reason bows submissively to His government, and the will yields an instant and humble compliance. Oh no! if He that is in the regenerate were not greater and more powerful than he that is in the world, such is the enmity of the heart to God, such the supreme control which Satan exerts over the whole empire of man, God would be forever shut out, and the soul forever lost. See how clearly regeneration is proved to be the work of the Spirit. God has written it as with a sunbeam, "that we are His workmanship,"[29] and that the Eternal Spirit is the mighty agent. (Winslow, Evening Thoughts, Jun 4)

---

29   Ephesians 2:10.

Reading: Job 25-26

The chief purport of Job's reply, in these words, seems to be directed to convince Bildad, that he had not answered, because he could not contradict what Job had advanced. And if Bildad thought, by what he had said, that he had benefitted God's cause, he was grossly mistaken. But, beside this, Job intimated also, that had Bildad been directed of God's Spirit, in this discourse, he would not only have taken notice of God's power, but of his grace; and especially as needed so much to be shewn to a poor afflicted creature, like Job. Now, said Job (for that seems the subject of his reply) if the Spirit of the Lord came to thee on this occasion, thou wouldest have seen how needful it is to comfort an afflicted soul, with spreading before him sweet views of God's love and grace; and not so much of his power, when the heart is before so dreadfully alarmed in the contemplation of his greatness. See a sweet precept to this purport, Isaiah 40:1, 2. (Hawker, Poor Man's Old Testament Commentary: Job-Psalms, 94)

Day 37

Reading: Job 27

"my lips will not speak unjustly, and my tongue will not utter deceit." Job 27:4

The opening of this sequel to Job's parable, carries with it the nature of an oath. It is a solemn asseveration of the truth. What Job means by God's taking away his judgment, if I apprehend right, intimates, that he himself (in consequence of his sharp exercises, and his ignorance at the same time of God's design), is prevented from forming a clear judgment, wherefore his soul is sore vexed. But, saith Job, let my God deal with me as seemeth him good; my faithfulness and integrity to him shall abide by me. Sweet and gracious determination, when a believing soul can and doth say, I know not how my God is leading me; but I know, that all his leadings are what they should be. Reader! see to it in your own experience, that path must be right which is marked out by infinite wisdom. And when our will is truly brought down to the Lord's will, then the soul cannot but approve, however unable to explain, all that the Lord is doing. (Hawker, Poor Man's Old Testament Commentary: Job-Psalms, 96–97)

Reading: Job 28

"Where then does wisdom come from, and where is understanding located?" Job 28:20

These are all so many sweet verses to the same effect. It should seem as if the mind of Job himself was so led out in the contemplation, that he knew not how to answer his own question, nor how to give it over unanswered. The manner in which he concludes gives the whole, if possible, more of a gospel form than anything which went before. By comparing scripture with scripture, as we are commanded, 1 Corinthians 2:13, we can best form our conclusions of the several expressions we meet with. Job saith in this place, that 'the fear of the Lord, that is wisdom; and to depart from evil is understanding.' Now as in other scriptures we are told, That the fear of the Lord is the beginning of wisdom; and that Christ is made of God, to us, wisdom; it should seem to follow, that in the knowledge of Christ, as the wisdom of God, for salvation, consists the whole of what is here expressed in this holy and childlike fear. I refer to those scriptures: 1 Corinthians 1:24, 30; Psalm 111:10; Jeremiah 32:40. And, as a collateral proof, the prophet Isaiah had it in commission to tell the Church, that the 'people of no understanding' would have no mercy nor favor shewn them: Isaiah 27:11. Is not this want of understanding an ignorance and despising of that wisdom of God in salvation by his dear Son? (Hawker, Poor Man's Old Testament Commentary: Job-Psalms, 103)

Reading: Job 29

"If only I could be as in months gone by ..." Job 29:2

Numbers of Christians can view the past with pleasure, but regard the present with dissatisfaction; they look back upon the days which they have passed in communing with the Lord as being the sweetest and the best they have ever known, but as to the present, it is clad in a sable garb of gloom and dreariness. Once they lived near to Jesus, but now they feel that they have wandered from him, and they say, "O that I were as in months past!" They complain that they have lost their evidences, or that they have not present peace of mind, or that they have no enjoyment in the means of grace, or that conscience is not so tender, or that they have not so much zeal for God's glory. The causes of this mournful state of things are manifold. It may arise through a comparative *neglect of prayer*, for a neglected closet is the beginning of all spiritual decline. Or it may be the result of *idolatry*. The heart has been occupied with something else, more than with God; the affections have been set on the things of earth, instead of the things of heaven. A jealous God will not be content with a divided heart; he must be loved first and best. He will withdraw the sunshine of his presence from a cold, wandering heart. Or the cause may be found in *self-confidence* and *self-righteousness*. Pride is busy in the heart, and self is exalted instead of lying low at the foot of the cross. Christian, if you are not now as you "were in months past," do not rest satisfied with *wishing* for a return of former happiness, but go at once to seek your Master, and tell him your sad state. Ask his grace and strength to help you to walk more closely with him; humble yourself before him, and he will lift you up, and give you yet again to enjoy the light of his countenance. Do not sit down to sigh and lament; while the beloved Physician lives there is hope, nay there is a certainty of recovery for the worst cases. (Spurgeon, Morning, Aug 11)

Reading: Job 30

My soul, behold in the sufferings of Job, what is, and deservedly ought to be, the lot of human nature. Born in sin, and therefore born to sorrow. *And shall a living man complain, a man for the punishment of his sins?* Job stands forth, in this instance, a living monument of what our nature, universally speaking, is exposed to. And but for the interposition of grace, in the mercy and love of God our Father, in giving his dear Son, and the Son of God in coming, and the Holy Spirit in bringing poor sinners acquainted with this rich salvation, all the temporal distresses of Job, aggravated by everlasting sorrows to have followed, would have been our portion forever. Oh! what shall we render to God for his mercies! *Thanks, thanks be unto God for his unspeakable gift!*[30]

But my soul, while contemplating the sorrows of Job, and the gracious interposition of heaven to soften and remove them, wilt thou not again and again look at Jesus; while reading Job's misery, and, in so lively a type of thy suffering Redeemer, feel all thy tender and affectionate powers going forth in love, and praise, and attachment, and obedience to thy blessed and adored Savior? Did Jesus, in the days of his flesh, endure the contradiction of sinners against himself, that his people might not be weary, and faint in mind? Oh! thou Lamb of God! how didst thou, in

30   2 Corinthians 9:15.

thy debased and low estate, submit to all indignities, griefs, sorrows, wounds, bruises! Who shall describe the dreadful pangs, and agonies like those of a travailing woman when bringing forth, in the garden and on the cross, the delivery of thy people from everlasting slavery and eternal death. Oh, precious God! thou shalt see the travail of thy soul, for so the Father promised, and be satisfied. Thou shalt justify many. The dew of thy birth shall be as the womb of the morning. And now, blessed Redeemer, having by thy death delivered thy redeemed from death, and by rising to life again having begotten them to everlasting life: now thou rememberest no more the anguish of thy travailing pains in redemption work, for joy that thy children are born into the world of grace, and shall hereafter be with thee in glory. Amen. (Hawker, Poor Man's Old Testament Commentary: Job-Psalms, 111)

Day 41

Reading: Job 31

"No stranger had to spend the night on the street, for I opened my door to the traveler." Job 31:32

Though Job was thus hospitable, yet we know that angels would have lodged in the street, if Lot had not taken them in. Nay, the Lord of angels, when he came a stranger upon earth, had not where to lay his head. He came indeed unto his own, but his own received him not. My soul, pause! hast thou done better by thy Lord? Nay, thou hast not. And though thou knowest the precept the apostle had it in commission to tell the church, not to be forgetful to entertain strangers, for thereby, as in the instance of the patriarch and others, some have entertained angels unawares; yet, my soul, how long did the Lord of life and glory stand without knocking at the door of thine heart, by the ministry of his word and ordinances, saying, "Open to me;" yea, and would have stood to this hour, had he not, by his own sovereign grace, put in his hand, by the hole of the door, and opened to himself. Oh, thou blissful stranger! didst thou, indeed, come from a far country, on this gracious, blessed errand, to seek and save that which was lost; and didst thou find every heart resolutely shut against thee? Didst thou, blessed Jesus, when travelling in the greatness of thy strength, open to thyself an entrance into the souls of thy people, by the sweet and constraining influences of thy holy Spirit? Do thou, then, almighty Lord, throw open the street-doors of my heart, for thy constant reception! Make them like the gates of that blessed city, which are never shut, day nor night. And cause my soul, like the prophet on the watch-tower, or Abraham in the tent door, to be always on the lookout for my Lord's approach, that I may invite thee, yea, constrain thee, to come in, and abide with me, and to make thyself known unto me, by the heart-burning discourses of thy word, and in breaking of bread, and of prayer. Yes, yes, thou glorious Traveler! who art perpetually on the visits of thy love, I do know thee; I do sometimes catch a sweet glimpse of thee, and trace the footsteps of thy grace, in thy word, in thy ordinances, and in the various ways by which thy presence is discoverable. Indeed, indeed, thou heavenly Stranger, thou shalt not lodge in the street; but I will take thee home to my house, to my heart and soul; and thou shalt sup with me, and I with thee, according to thine own most gracious promise, and I will cause thee to drink of spiced wine, of the juice of my pomegranate. (Hawker, The Poor Man's Morning Portion, Jul 24)

Reading: Job 32

The whole of these verses seems to be but as the preface to Elihu's discourse. He bespeaks the favor of his hearers, and apologizeth for what he might offer; but, to conciliate their minds, he tells them, that he is bursting to deliver what he had to say, so important it is in his view. The frame of mind in Elihu, and the earnestness he felt to be useful in this controversy, may serve to teach how much a soul that is full of Jesus, and longs to go forth in his name and salvation, for the good of others, may be supposed to feel in his labor of love. To be shut up in a corner, and prohibited from speaking of the Lord, when we see souls perishing for lack of knowledge, what a grief must this be to faithful servants of the Lord Jesus! Jeremiah describes his state under this affliction, and saith, That the word of the Lord was in his heart, *as a burning fire shut up in his bones, so that he was weary with forbearing, and could not stay.*[31] (Hawker, Poor Man's Old Testament Commentary: Job-Psalms, 119)

---

31   Jeremiah 20:9.

Day 43

Reading: Job 33

"He will look at men and say, "I have sinned and perverted what was right; yet I did not get what I deserved. He redeemed my soul from going down to the Pit, and I will continue to see the light."" Job 33:27-28

Let the child of God be encouraged to take all his sins to his heavenly Father. Have you sinned? Have you taken a single step in departure from God? Is there the slightest consciousness of guilt? Go at once to the throne of grace; stay not until you find some secret place for confession-stay not until you are alone; lift up your heart at once to God, and confess your sin with the hand of faith upon the great, atoning Sacrifice. Open all your heart to Him. Do not be afraid of a full and honest confession. Shrink not from unfolding its most secret recesses – lay all bare before His eyes. Do you think He will turn from the exposure? Do you think He will close His ear against your breathings? Oh no! Listen to His own encouraging, persuasive declarations – "Go and proclaim these words towards the north, and say, Return, you backsliding Israel, says the Lord; and I will not cause mine anger to fall upon you: for I am merciful, says the Lord; and I will not keep anger forever. Only acknowledge your iniquity that you have transgressed against the Lord your God."[32] "I will heal their backsliding; I will love

32   Jeremiah 3:11-13.

them freely; for mine anger is turned away from him."[33] Oh, what words are these! Does the eye of the poor backslider fall on this page? And as he now reads of God's readiness to pardon – of God's willingness to receive back the repenting prodigal – of His yearning after His wandering child – feels his heart melted, his soul subdued, and, struck with that amazing declaration, "Only acknowledge your iniquity," would dare creep down at His feet, and weep, and mourn, and confess. Oh! Is there one such now reading this page? Then return, my brother, return! God – the God against whom you have sinned – says, "Return." Your Father – the Father from whom you have wandered – is looking out for the first return of your soul, for the first kindling of godly sorrow, for the first confession of sin. God has not turned His back upon you, though you have turned your back upon Him. God has not forgotten to be gracious, though you have forgotten to be faithful. "I remember you" – is His own touching language – "the kindness of your youth, the love of your espousals." Oh! then, come back; this moment, come back; the fountain is still open – Jesus is still the same – the blessed and eternal Spirit, loving and faithful as ever – God ready for pardon: take up, then, the language of the prodigal and say, "I will arise and go to my Father, and will say unto him, Father, I have sinned against heaven and in Your sight, and am no more worthy to be called Your son."[34] "If we confess our sins, He is faithful and just to forgive us our sins, and to cleanse us from all unrighteousness."[35]

---

33   Hosea 14:4.
34   Luke 15:18-19.
35   1 John 1:9.

The blessings that result from a strict observance of daily confession of sin are rich and varied. We would from the many specify two. The conscience retains its tender susceptibility of guilt. Just as a breath will tarnish a mirror highly polished, so will the slightest aberration of the heart from God – the smallest sin – leave its impression upon a conscience in the habit of a daily unburdening itself in confession, and of a daily washing in the fountain. Going thus to God, and acknowledging iniquity over the head of Immanuel – pleading the atoning blood – the conscience retains its tenderness, and sin, all sin, is viewed as that which God hates, and the soul abhors.

This habit, too, keeps, so to speak, a clear account between God and the believer. Sins daily and hourly committed are not forgotten; they fade not from the mind, and therefore they need not the correcting rod to recall them to remembrance. For let us not forget, God will eventually bring our sins to remembrance; "He will call to remembrance the iniquity." David had forgotten his sin against God, and his treacherous conduct to Uriah, until God sent the prophet Nathan to bring his iniquity to remembrance. A daily confession, then, of sin, a daily washing in the fountain, will preserve the believer from many and, perhaps, deep afflictions. This was David's testimony – "I acknowledged my sin unto You, and mine iniquity have I not hid. I said, I will confess my transgression unto the Lord, and You forgave the iniquity of my sin."[36] (Winslow, Evening Thoughts, Oct 15)

---

36   Psalm 32:5.

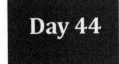

Reading: Job 34

"Suppose someone says to God, "I have endured my punishment; I will no longer act wickedly. Teach me what I cannot see; if I have done wrong, I won't do it again."" Job 34:31-32

Oh, what a detector of the secret state of our souls does the season of trial often prove! We are not aware of our impaired strength, of our weak faith, of our powerless grace – how feeble our hold on Christ is – how legal our views of the gospel are – how beclouded our minds may be – how partial our acquaintance with God is – until we are led into the path of trouble. The season of prosperity veils the real state of our souls from our view. No Christian can form an accurate estimate of his spiritual condition, who has not been brought into a state of trial. We faint in the day of adversity, because we then find – what, perhaps, was not even suspected in the day of prosperity – that our strength is small.

But seasons of trial are emphatically what the word expresses – they try the work in the souls of the righteous. The inner life derives immense advantage from them. The deeper discovery that is then made of the evil of the heart is not the least important result: "Foolishness is bound in the heart of a child; but the rod of correction shall drive it far from him."[37] What

---

37   Proverbs 22:15.

folly still dwells in the hearts of the wise – bound up and half concealed – who can tell? Who would have suspected such developments in the life of Abraham, of David, of Solomon, of Peter? And so is it with all who yet are the possessors of that wisdom which will guide their souls to eternal glory. Folly is bound up in their hearts; but the sanctified rod of correction reveals it, and the discovery proves one of the costliest blessings in the experience of the disciplined child. Listen to the language of Moses, addressed to the children of Israel: "You shall remember all the way which the Lord your God led you these forty years in the wilderness, to humble you, and to prove you, to know what was in your heart, whether you would keep His commandments or no."[38] And oh, what a discovery that forty years' marching and counter-marching in the wilderness was to them of the pride, and impatience, and unbelief, and ingratitude, and distrust that were bound up in their heart! And yet, though all this evil was deep-seated in their nature, they knew it not, and suspected it not, until trial brought it to the surface. Thus, beloved, is it with us. The latent evil is brought to light. God leaves us to try what is in our heart, and this may be the first step in the reviving of His gracious work in our souls. Oh, let us not, then, shrink from the probing, nor startle at its discovery, if it but lead us nearer to holiness, nearer to Christ, nearer to God, nearer to heaven!

The time of trouble is often, too, a, time of remembrance and so becomes a time of reviving. Past backslidings – unthought of, unsuspected, and unconfessed – are recalled to memory in the season

38   Deuteronomy 8:2.

that God is dealing with us. David had forgotten his transgression, and the brethren of Joseph their sin, until trouble summoned it back to memory. Times of trial are searching times, remembering times. Then with David we exclaim, "I thought on my ways, and turned my feet unto Your testimonies: I made haste, and delayed not to keep Your commandments."[39] (Winslow, Evening Thoughts, Jan 25)

---

39   Psalm 119:59-60.

Day 45

Reading: Job 35

"But no one asks, "Where is God my Maker, who provides us with songs in the night,"" Job 35:10

Who but God could give songs in the night? No saint on earth, no angel in heaven, has power to tune our hearts to a single note of praise in the hour of their grief; no, nor could any creature above or below breathe a word of comfort, of hope, or of support, when heart and flesh were failing. Who but the incarnate God has power enough, or love enough, or sympathy enough, to come and embosom Himself in our very circumstances-to enter into the very heart of our sorrow – to go down into the deepest depth of our woe, and strike a chord there that, responding to His touch, shall send forth a more than angel's music? It is God who gives these songs. He is acquainted with your sorrows: He regards your night of weeping: He knows the way that you take. He may be lost to your view, but you cannot be lost to His. The darkness of your night – grief may veil Him from your eye, but the "darkness and the light are both alike to Him."[40] Then repair to Him for your song. Ask Him so to sanctify your sorrow by His grace, and so to comfort it by His Spirit, and so to glorify Himself in your patient endurance of it, and so to make you to know the why of your trial, and your trial so to <u>answer the</u> mission on which it was sent, as will

40   Psalm 139:12.

enable you to raise this note of praise – "You have turned for me my mourning into dancing: You have put off my sackcloth, and girded me with gladness; to the end that my glory may sing praise to You, and not be silent."[41]

In giving you a throne of grace, God has given you a song, methinks, one of the sweetest ever sung in the house of our pilgrimage. To feel that we have a God who hears and answers prayer – who has done so in countless instances, and is prepared still to give us at all times an audience – oh! The unutterable blessings of this truth. Sing aloud then, you sorrowful saints; for great and precious is your privilege of communion with God. In the night of your every grief, and trial, and difficulty, do not forget that in your lowest frame you may sing this song – "Having boldness to enter into the holiest by the blood of Jesus, by a new and living way, I will draw near, and pour out my heart to God."[42] Chant, then, His high praises as you pass along, that there is a place where you may disclose every need, repose every sorrow, deposit every burden, breathe every sigh, and lose yourself in communion with God – that place is the blood-besprinkled mercy-seat, of which God says, "There will I meet with you, and I will commune with you."[43]

Ah! But perhaps you exclaim, "Would that I could sing! I can weep, and moan, and even trust, but I cannot rejoice." Yes, but there is One who can give even you, beloved, a song in the night. Place your harp in His hands, all broken and unstrung as it is,

41   Psalm 30:11.
42   Hebrews 10:19-22.
43   Exodus 25:22.

and He will repair and retune it; and then, breathing upon it His Spirit, and touching it with His own gentle hand, that heart, that was so sad and joyless, shall yet sing the high praises of its God. How much of God's greatness and glory in nature is concealed until the night reveals it! The sun is withdrawn, twilight disappears, and darkness robes the earth. Then appears the brilliant firmament, studded and glowing with myriads of constellations! Oh, the indescribable wonder, the surpassing glory, of that scene! But it was the darkness that brought it all to view; thus, is it in the Christian's life. How much of God would be unseen, how much of His glory concealed, how little should we know of Jesus, but for the night-season of mental darkness and of heart-sorrow. The sun that shone so cheeringly has set; the grey twilight that looked so pensively has disappeared; and just as the night of woe set in, filling you with trembling, with anxiety, and with fear, a scene of overpowering grandeur suddenly bursts upon the astonished eye of your faith. The glory of God, as your Father, has appeared-the character of Jesus, as a loving tender Brother, has unfolded – the Spirit, as a Comforter, has whispered – your interest in the great redemption has been revealed – and a new earth redolent with a thousand sweets, and a new heaven resplendent with countless suns, has floated before your view. It was the darkness of your night of sorrow that made visible all this wonder and all this glory; and but for that sorrow how little would you have known of it. "I will sing of mercy and of judgment: unto You, O Lord, will I sing."[44]

---

44   Psalm 101:1.

Suffering, sorrowful believer! Pluck your harp from your willow, and, with the hand of faith and love, sweep it to the high praises of your God. Praise Him for Himself – praise Him for Jesus – praise Him for conversion – praise Him for joys – praise Him for sorrows – praise Him for chastenings – praise Him for the hope of glory – oh praise Him for all! Thus, singing the Lord's song in a strange land, you will be learning to sing it in diviner sounds –

"With those just spirits that wear victorious palms,

Hymns devout, and holy psalms

Singing everlastingly."

"And they sing the song of Moses, the servant of God, and the song of the Lamb, saying, Great and marvelous are Your works, Lord God almighty; just and true are Your ways, O King of saints. Who shall not fear You, O Lord, and glorify Your name? For You only are holy: for all nations shall come and worship before You."[45] (Winslow, Evening Thoughts, Sep 4)

---

45   Revelation 15:3-4.

Day 46

Reading: Job 36

"Yes, God is exalted beyond our knowledge; the number of his years cannot be counted." Job 36:26

There is a state of mind often enfeebling to the exercise of prayer, arising from the difficulty of forming proper views of the spiritual nature of the Divine object of prayer. The spirituality of God, through the weakness of our nature, has been felt to be, by some, a stumbling-block in the approach of the soul. "God is a Spirit,"[46] is a solemn announcement that meets it at the very threshold, and so completely overawes and abashes the mind, as to congeal every current of thought and of feeling, and well-near to crush the soul with its inconceivable idea. Nor is this surprising. Prayer is the approach of finite to Infinity; and although it is the communing of spirit with Spirit, yet it is the finite communing with the Infinite and that through the organs of sense. Is it any marvel, then, that at periods a believer should be baffled in his endeavor to form some just conception of the Divine existence, some faint idea of the nature of that God to whom his soul addresses itself; and, failing in the attempt, should turn away in sadness, sorrow, and despair?

The remedy for this state of mind, we believe, is at hand. It is simply scriptural. That we can enlarge

---

46   John 4:24.

our thoughts with any adequate idea of the nature and the appearance of the Divine Spirit is an utter impossibility. He that attempts it, and thinks he has succeeded, lives in the region of fancy, and opposes himself to the revelation of God Himself, which expressly declares, "No man has seen God at any time."[47] "Who only has immortality, dwelling in the light which no man can approach unto; whom no man has seen, nor can see."[48] This being then admitted, as it must be by all reflective minds, the question arises, "How am I to view God? What idea am I to form of His existence in approaching Him in prayer?" In reply, two things are necessary in getting proper thoughts of God as the object of prayer. First, that the mind should resign all its attempts to comprehend the mode of the Divine existence, and should concentrate all its powers upon the contemplation of the character of the Divine existence. In what relation God stands to the creature, not in what way He exists in Himself, but is the point with which we have to do in approaching Him. Let the mind be wrapped in devout contemplations of His holiness, benevolence, love, truth, wisdom, justice, &c., and there will be no room for vain and fruitless imaginations respecting the fathomless and inconceivable mode of His existence. The second thing necessary is that the mind should view God in Christ. (Winslow, Evening Thoughts, Apr 1)

---

47   John 1:18; John 6:46; 1 John 4:12.

48   1 Timothy 6:16.

Day 47

Reading: Job 37

Here are the same traces of God's power pointed to, in the effect and operation of winds, and their constant ministration, by his appointment. All which, were our minds not dullness itself, would unceasingly lead us to the contemplation of God. Perhaps there is not a subject so general among all ranks and orders of people, as that of weather. It becomes the usual subject as we pass the street, or in the house; what a fine day, or what a rainy day, it is today. But how seldom do we hear serious observations added to the conversation, how gracious the Lord is in the appointment. Reader, let you and I never converse on the weather without connecting with it our humble and devout acknowledgment of Him and his mercy, in the different appointments of the weather, who gathereth the winds (as the wise man expresseth it) in his fists, and hath bounded the waters in his garment. Prov. 30:4. And, in a more spiritual sense, let the winds of the north, and the south, here spoken of, lead our minds to the recollection of the divine breathing of the Holy Spirit, concerning whose gracious operations upon the hearts of his people, the Redeemer calls for the manifestation of his blessed office, in desiring the north wind, and the south wind, to blow upon the garden, which is the church of Jesus, that the spices may flow; and that then the Church's beloved, even

Jesus himself, will come into his garden, and eat of his pleasant fruits. Song 4:16. (Hawker, Poor Man's Old Testament Commentary: Job-Psalms, 136–137)

Day 48

Reading: Job 38

"Can you fasten the chains of the Pleiades or loosen the belt of Orion?" Job 38:31

If inclined to boast of our abilities, the grandeur of nature may soon show us how puny we are. We cannot move the least of all the twinkling stars, or quench so much as one of the beams of the morning. We speak of power, but the heavens laugh us to scorn. When the Pleiades shine forth in spring with vernal joy we cannot restrain their influences, and when Orion reigns aloft, and the year is bound in winter's fetters, we cannot relax the icy bands. The seasons revolve according to the divine appointment, neither can the whole race of men effect a change therein. Lord, what is man?

In the spiritual, as in the natural world, man's power is limited on all hands. When the Holy Spirit sheds abroad his delights in the soul, none can disturb; all the cunning and malice of men are ineffectual to stay the genial quickening power of the Comforter. When he deigns to visit a church and revive it, the most inveterate enemies cannot resist the good work; they may ridicule it, but they can no more restrain it than they can push back the spring when the Pleiades rule the hour. God wills it, and so it must be. On the other hand, if the Lord in sovereignty, or in justice, bind up a man so that he is in soul bondage, who can give him liberty? He alone can remove the winter of spiritual death from an individual or a people. He looses the bands of Orion, and none but he. What a blessing it is that he can do it. O that he would perform the wonder tonight. Lord, end my winter, and let my spring begin. I cannot with all my longings raise my soul out of her death and dullness, but all things are possible with thee. I need celestial influences, the clear shinings of thy love, the beams of thy grace, the light of thy countenance, these are the Pleiades to me. I suffer much from sin and temptation, these are my wintry signs, my terrible Orion. Lord, work wonders in me, and for me. Amen. (Spurgeon, Eve, Mar 21)

Day 49

Reading: Job 39

Reader, let you and I, in the perusal of this chapter of God's tender mercies over all his works, draw the same conclusion from the review of so much love, as the Apostle did on another occasion, and say, *Doth God take care for oxen, or saith he it altogether for our sakes?* Doth God so clothe the grass of the field (saith our adorable Redeemer when admonishing his people to cast all their care upon God, who careth for them)[49] which today is, and tomorrow is cast into the oven? Precious Lord; in the view of such things let our souls be firmly, fully, faithfully established in the unalterable assurance, that in Jesus all our interests are secured; all our concerns are everlastingly provided for. What is there that a believer in Jesus should be anxious about? Hath he not Christ for his portion; and can he fail when anchored here? Can he miscarry when Jesus himself hath said, *Because I live, ye shall live also?*[50] Reader, oh for faith, in lively exercise to hang upon a Covenant God in Christ, when the outward circumstances of visible comforts seemed dying; for this is the very moment for the exercise. Had Job uniformly done this, and when the streams failed, in sensible comforts, had he removed to the fountain head, he would have found a Covenant God in Christ, whom he knew, and had professed to be his kinsman-

---

49   Matthew 6:25-34; 1 Peter 5:7.
50   John 14:19.

Redeemer, sufficient to have borne him all the way through. Reader, let you and I derive this sweet and blessed conclusion from what the Lord hath so conclusively set forth in this chapter. He that caters for the birds of the air; He that affords suited strength to the wild goats of the rock in bringing forth; that provides against the silly unconcern of the ostrich, and the unthinking horse in the battle; He will never be less provident to his own children, that call upon him. They are the gift of his love to his dear Son! they are the purchase of his Son's blood! they are the objects of his grace, and brought under the quickening influence, and divine teaching, of his blessed Spirit; and therefore he will arrange and direct all things for his glory and their welfare. They are brought within a wise appointed covenant, ordered in all things, and sure: they are under his own wise providence; they are encompassed with exceeding great and precious promises; and, to crown all, God is a faithful God, and a sure Covenant God in Christ. Hence begone, I would say, all doubts, all fears, all misgivings. Let nothing so unbecoming in me, and so dishonorable to my God, for a moment arise in my mind. Let creatures die; let all my substance, like Job's, be wasted; if my God sees it fit, it must be wise, it must be right. Jesus lives, and that's enough. Oh! how sweet his words: 'Am I not better to thee than ten sons?' Yes, precious Lord! thou art indeed in the place of millions of creature-joys; for millions without thee would be nothing; and having thee, I have all things: my joy here, and my portion forever. (Hawker, Poor Man's Old Testament Commentary: Job-Psalms, 147-148)

Day 50

Reading: Job 40

"Behold, I am vile ..." Job 40:4 (AKJV)

One cheering word, poor lost sinner, for thee! You think you must not come to God because you are vile. Now, there is not a saint living on earth but has been made to feel that he is vile. If Job, and Isaiah, and Paul were all obliged to say "I am vile," oh, poor sinner, wilt thou be ashamed to join in the same confession? If divine grace does not eradicate all sin from the believer, how dost thou hope to do it thyself? and if God loves his people while they are yet vile, dost thou think thy vileness will prevent his loving thee? Believe on Jesus, thou outcast of the world's society! Jesus calls *thee*, and such as thou art.

> *"Not the righteous, not the righteous;*
> *Sinners, Jesus came to call."*

Even now say, "Thou hast died for sinners; I am a sinner, Lord Jesus, sprinkle thy blood on me;" if thou wilt confess thy sin thou shalt find pardon. If, now, with all thy heart, thou wilt say, "I am vile, wash me," thou shalt be washed now. If the Holy Spirit shall enable thee from thy heart to cry

> *"Just as I am, without one plea*
> *But that thy blood was shed for me,*
> *And that thou bidd'st me come to thee,*
> *O Lamb of God, I come!"*

thou shalt rise from reading this morning's portion with all thy sins pardoned; and though thou didst wake this morning with every sin that man hath ever committed on thy head, thou shalt rest tonight accepted in the Beloved; though once degraded with the rags of sin, thou shalt be adorned with a robe of righteousness, and appear white as the angels are. For "now," mark it, "*Now* is the accepted time." If thou "believest on him who justifieth the ungodly thou art saved." Oh! may the Holy Spirit give thee saving faith in him who receives the vilest. (Spurgeon, Morning, Jun 6)

Day 51

Reading: Job 41

I stay not to offer any comment upon this description of the Leviathan, neither shall I enter into an enquiry what animal it is that is here intended by the Leviathan: some have thought that it is the crocodile that is meant to be described; and others conceive that it is the whale: but it appears to me to be of little importance to inquire. It is sufficient that it is a creature of God, and, as such, displays in its formation God's power and sovereignty. And the conclusion to be made from the view of such a wonderful production, is best made in the words of God himself: 'If a man would tremble at the idea of stirring up such a creature, who can be able to stand before God? If the thing created be tremendous, what must the great Creator be?'

The description here given of the Leviathan is most striking and magnificent. How beautifully the several features of this vast creature is set forth; how grand and lofty the account of him. But after all that is said of the strength and majesty of the Leviathan, the only creature in God's creation that is said to be made without fear, the highest possible representation of created greatness, yet when we call to mind, that this huge animal lies at the mercy of God, and is as easily destroyed by his Maker as the smallest fly or worm, how astonishingly great and powerful must be the Lord Jehovah; and what an argument ariseth herefrom, both to humble us to the dust of the earth, in token of our nothingness, before the Lord; and, above all things, to seek his favor, *in whose hand all our breath is, and whose are all our ways.*[51] (Hawker, Poor Man's Old Testament Commentary: Job-Psalms, 152–154)

---

51   Daniel 5:23.

Day 52

Reading: Job 42

"I had heard reports about you, but now my eyes have seen you." Job 42:5

And now, farewell Job. We have seen, in thy most instructive history, the blessed truth confirmed, that the end of the Lord, in the events of his servants' ministry and lives upon earth, is very pitiful and gracious. Sweetly, under the Holy Spirit's divine teaching, do we learn from hence, that the Lord is righteous in all his ways, and holy in all his works; and especially in the lives of his servants, that he ordereth and arrangeth all things as shall best promote his gracious designs in the furtherance of his own glory and his people's happiness. Satan may be permitted to exercise a certain degree of power; but how painful soever this may be, during the operation, to flesh and blood, the whole must and shall minister to the enemy's disgrace, to God's faithful servants comfort, and to the display of the divine wisdom, love, and goodness. No temptation shall overtake them but what is common to man, and with every temptation the Lord will make a way to escape, until at length *the God of peace will bruise Satan under their feet.*[52]

But before I take a last farewell of Job, let me look once more, and behold in how many things he bore

---

52   Romans 16:20.

a striking resemblance to my adorable Redeemer. Yes, thou blessed man of Uz, surely the Holy Spirit graciously intended to teach the Church, in thy history, somewhat, however faint in the outlines, of what the Church for ever must be delighted to dwell upon; of Him who is the first and last, and never-ceasing object of her affection. Was Job the greatest man of all the East? And what was Jesus, the wisdom-man, set up from everlasting, but the greatest of all, and Lord of all, that in all things he might have the preeminency? Was Job perfect and upright before God, one that feared God, and eschewed evil? And what wert thou, thou blessed Jesus, in thy human nature, but holy, harmless, and undefiled, separate from sinners, and made higher than the heavens? Was Job suddenly brought from a state of affluence to a state of poverty and sorrow? And can we overlook thee, thou adorable Lord Jesus, who, though rich, yet for our sakes didst become poor, that we through thy poverty might be made rich? Did Satan assault Job in his affliction, and buffet him in every direction? And can we forget thine unequalled temptations, O thou Prince of Sufferers, when from the river Jordan to the garden, and the cross, Satan furiously made his attack on thee, though in thy holy nature he could find no part vulnerable to his fiery darts? But oh! precious Jesus, what were the conflicts of the man of Uz compared to thine thou man of sorrows, and acquainted with grief? What persecution, from false friends, in Job's history, can bear resemblance to thine, when thou enduredst such a contradiction of sinners against thyself, lest thy people should be weary and faint in their minds? Many of thy faithful servants, through thy grace enabling them, have done virtuously, but thou excellest them all. Yes, blessed Jesus! in all things it becometh thee to have the pre-eminence, in suffering as in glory, that thou mightest be *the first-born among many brethren.*[53] It is sweet and precious to follow the teachings of the Holy Spirit, and to trace, in the lives of thy people, in those early ages of thy Church, any outlines of character as typical of thee. It is highly profitable to eye Job shadowing forth some faint resemblance of thee in his original greatness, with which his history begins! in his humiliation, in his interceding for his friends, and in his final exaltation. But oh! blessed Lord, enable me to look through all these shades to thy bright manifestations, when coming from thy glory in heaven, and tabernacling upon earth in substance of our flesh, thou didst pass through sorrows, sufferings, reproaches, persecution; bearing our sins in thine own body on the tree, and dying the just for the unjust, to bring us unto God. Hail, thou Almighty Jesus! now hath God our Father turned thy captivity, and blessed thee above thy fellows. Now hath he constituted and appointed thee as the Great High Priest and Intercessor for all thy redeemed; and thee, and them in thee, he accepts. And now hath he given thee a family of both Jew and Gentile, to bless thy name, to sing thy praise, and to adore thee forever. And now shall every knee bend before thee, and every tongue confess, that Jesus Christ is Lord, to the glory of God the Father.[54]

I cannot close this part of my feeble labors,

53   Romans 8:29.
54   Philippians 2:10-11; Romans 14:11.

without desiring to fall down before the mercy seat in thankfulness for such distinguishing mercy as hath been manifested in permitting so unhallowed a pen to be thus employed, imploring pardon and forgiveness for all that is here offered. I find cause, at every review, to take shame in the consciousness how far, how very far short it comes of the divine original. Blessed Master, I would say, manifest thine accustomed compassion to the errors of this humble work. Preserve all that read it from injury in the perusal: and, if it shall please thee to commission it for good but to one of thine, to the sovereignty of thy grace shall be all the glory, in condescending to make use of so poor an instrument to so great a service, *to work in thy people both to will and to do according to thy good pleasure.*[55] (Hawker, Poor Man's Old Testament Commentary: Job-Psalms, 158–159)

---

55   Philippians 2:13.

Day 53

Reading: Genesis 12

"So Abram went, as the LORD had told him ..." Genesis 12:4

Methinks I would not read this call of God to Abram, and observe the Patriarch's ready faith to obey it, without begging grace from God, to attend to the many precious invitations with which I am called upon to follow Jesus in the regeneration; and, like Abram, to arise, leave house and home, and kindred, and relations; and by faith become *the follower of them who now through faith and patience inherit the promises.*[56] And oh! that He, who endued the patriarch with such holy fortitude, would arm my mind with the like confidence, that, amidst every discouragement, *against hope I might believe in hope;*[57] and trust God, where I cannot trace him. Dearest Jesus! grant me as thou didst the patriarch, the frequent visits of thy love, and then whatever famine shall arise, or straits surround me, in the midst of all, a wilderness with thee will, to my soul, be far preferable to a land flowing with milk and honey without thee! (Hawker, Poor Man's Old Testament Commentary: Genesis-Numbers, 52-53)

---

56   Hebrews 6:12.
57   Romans 4:18.

Reading: Genesis 13

"... Look from the place where you are ..." Genesis 13:14

Amidst all the competitions, strifes and jealousies, which this world's goods excites among men in life, let Abram's portion be my portion. Let me but be able, in a well-grounded assurance to call Jesus mine, and I value not what sinners value of the perishing things of time and sense. Precious Redeemer! it is thy favor which gives a sweetness to every joy, and softens every sorrow. Let the cisterns of all creature-comforts be dried up, if thy, wisdom see it fit: the streams of thine everlasting love will still flow. And while, like the prophet, I can truly *rejoice in the Lord, and joy in the God of my salvation*, it matters not, *even if the fig tree doth not blossom, neither fruit be in the vines.*[58]

Methinks this gracious call of God to Abram, which is always sweet in mercy, is uncommonly so in this instance: *lift up thine eyes, and look from the place where thou art.* And is not the same in effect said to every believer? Lift up thine eyes, and behold in, every direction, northward, and southward, and eastward, and westward, how all mercies and promises are confirmed to the faithful, in the Covenant of grace which is in Christ Jesus. *All are*

---

58   Habakkuk 3:17-18.

yours saith the Apostle if ye are Christ's; whether the world, or life, or death, or things present, or things to come. Blessed God! May it be my mercy to enjoy all things in Jesus, and Jesus in all things! (Hawker, Poor Man's Old Testament Commentary: Genesis-Numbers, 55-56)

Reading: Genesis 14

"Melchizedek, king of Salem, brought out bread and wine; he was a priest to God Most High." Genesis 14:18

Was it not in the evening of the day, when Abraham, returning from the slaughter of the kings, met this illustrious person? And will Jesus, my Melchisedek, meet and bless me in the evening of this day, after my return from conflicts, trials, and exercises? I would fain indulge the sweet thought. Surely this Melchisedek could be no other than Jesus. And did he love his people then—and doth he not love them now? Did Jesus witness their battles, and come forth and refresh them? And is he not Jesus still? Sit down, my soul, and attend to what the Holy Spirit saith of this Melchisedek; and see whether, through his teaching, thou canst make no discoveries of Jesus. Was this Melchisedek priest of the most high God? And who but the Son of God was ever sworn into this office with an oath? Was Melchisedek a priest for ever? Who but Jesus was this? Had Melchisedek neither beginning of days nor end of life? And who but Jesus is the first and the last? Was Melchisedek without father, without mother? And who of Jesus shall declare his generation? Did Melchisedek bless the great father of the faithful? And hath not God the Father sent his Son to bless us, in turning away every one of us from our iniquities? Did the king of Salem bring forth bread and wine, to refresh the Patriarch and his people? And doth not our King of righteousness bring forth at his supper the same, as memorials of his love? yea, his own precious body, which is meat indeed, and his blood drink indeed. Precious Jesus, thou great Melchisedek! bring forth anew, this night, these tokens of thy love. Make thyself known to me in breaking of bread and prayer. And whilst thou art imparting to me most blessed views of thyself, give me to apprehend and know thee, and richly enjoy thy soul-strengthening, soul-comforting presence. And oh! for grace from thee, Lord, and the sweet influences of thine Holy Spirit; that, like the Patriarch Abraham, I may give thee tithes of all I possess! It is true, I have nothing, and am nothing; yea, in myself, am worse than nothing. But of thine own would I give thee. Like the poor widow in the gospel, I would cast all my living into thy treasury. The two mites, which make a farthing, my soul and body, do I give unto thee. And those are both thine, by creation, by gift, by purchase, and by the conquest of thy grace. Take, therefore, all; and enable me to present my soul and body a living sacrifice, holy, acceptable unto the Lord, which is my reasonable service. (Hawker, The Poor Man's Evening Portion, Jan 5)

Reading: Genesis 15

"Abram believed the LORD, and he credited it to him as righteousness." Genesis 15:6

Let the visions of God with Abram have this effect upon all the true seed of Abram, earnestly to desire and as highly to prize, all the gracious manifestations of the divine love. May we esteem all the ordinances and means of grace, which tend to open a channel of communication between God and our souls. But yet more affectionately covet communion with the God of ordinances. Blessed Jesus! I would say, both for myself and for the Reader, Oh! do thou manifest thyself unto me otherwise than thou dost unto the world! May I know that thou art my portion, my shield, and my exceeding great reward.

Reader! behold the Patriarch Abram, and learn in his history the sweetness of exercised faith. Amidst all those precious promises of a faithful God, yet how long, how seemingly tedious and trying, the dispensation was appointed to be to his seed, before the fulfillment. Oh! for faith, that against hope, you and I may believe in hope; and in all our trials, *may we run with patience the race that is set before us, looking unto Jesus the author and finisher of our faith.*[59] And as the Patriarch considered himself as sojourning in a strange country, and was looking

59   Hebrews 12:1-2.

beyond the tabernacles which he inhabited, for a *city which had foundations,*[60] so may we never lose sight of that most certain truth, that *here we have no continuing city,* but may we be *seeking one to come.* And oh! thou Almighty giver of faith, increase our faith, and enable us to *walk by faith,* and not by sight, until we realize the divine presence in all the glories of eternity, and *receive the end of our faith, even the salvation of our souls.* (Hawker, Poor Man's Old Testament Commentary: Genesis-Numbers, 63)

---

60   Hebrews 11:10.

Day 57

Reading: Genesis 16

"So she named the LORD who spoke to her: "You are El-roi," for she said, "In this place, have I actually seen the one who sees me?" That is why the well is called Beer-lahai-roi ..." Genesis 16:13, 14.

Behold, my soul, what very blessed instructions arise out of this scripture. Beg of God the Holy Spirit to make thy present evening meditation of it sweet. The words themselves are the reflection of *Hagar*, the handmaid of *Sarah*, when she fled from her mistress into the wilderness. In a situation of great distress, the Lord manifested himself to her, and the conclusion she drew from it was, as is expressed, "Thou God seest me." This, indeed, was the name she gave unto the Lord, as if henceforth she would know the Lord in all his mercies by this name. Sweet thought! Jesus is known by his name, and in his name his grace is revealed. But Hagar added another delightful reflection, "for she said, Have I also here looked after him that seeth me?" As if she had said, "And hath the grace of God, looking upon me, wrought grace in me?" But the words may be read differently, and some indeed read them so: "Have I looked for the Lord, when the Lord looked after me?" "Alas! I thought not of him until that he called me by his grace." Here is another delightful thought of Hagar's, and in perfect harmony with the gospel of

Jesus. "For if we love God, it is because he first loved us."[61] And there is another reflection as interesting as either: "Wherefore the well was called Beer-lahai-roi;" that is, "the well of him that liveth and looketh on." This became Hagar's memorial, as if she would forever perpetuate the name of Him that looked on and regarded her sorrow. This well, this place, this sacred spot, shall be Hagar's Bethel! It shall tell everyone that passeth by, Here the Lord wrought, and here he manifested grace to a poor handmaid. Precious scripture of a precious God! Who but must feel delight in beholding Hagar's faith? And who but must find cause to bless God, both for giving that faith, and affording so favorable an occasion for the exercise of if? And shall I not, and will not you, reader, gather some of the many delightful instructions from it, for our own use, which it is so highly calculated to bring? Did the angel of the Lord look on Hagar, and doth he not look on every child of his? Am I at any time looking after Jesus, and is not Jesus looking after me? Oh! what a volume of encouragement ariseth from this one view, to persevere in looking after him and in waiting for him! that before I thought of him, or was looking after him, Jesus was both caring and looking upon me! It is impossible to be beforehand with God. Put down, then, my soul, this conclusion from this blessed scripture, that in every place, in every state, upon every occasion, thy Jesus liveth, and looketh on. And do thou call thy Lord by the same name as Hagar did, that speaketh to thee in every place, and by every providence, "Thou God seest me." And never, never forget, when thou art hardest

------

61   1 John 4:19.

put to it, and art seeking Jesus, sorrowing, though to thy blind eye he doth not so immediately appear, yet he is still seeing and following thee, even when thou art not seeking and following after him. Let this be in thy constant remembrance: and make every spot that is memorable like the well *Beer-lahai-roi*, to draw water of salvation from; for in every one it is the well of Him that liveth, and looketh on. Precious Lord Jesus! henceforth grant me grace, that while thou art looking after me with love and favor, I may be looking unto thee with faith and praise. And through every step of my wilderness state, while going home to my Father's house, let this be my comfort and the burden of my song in this house of my pilgrimage, "Thou God seest me." (Hawker, The Poor Man's Evening Portion, Mar 4)

Day 58

Reading: Genesis 17

"... It is a permanent covenant to be your God and the God of your offspring after you." Genesis 17:7

My Christian Brother [or Sister]! Are *you* included in this blessed Covenant? Have *you* the marks and characters of it? Can you say as *Paul* did, We are *the true circumcision, which worship God in spirit; rejoice in Christ Jesus; and have no confidence in the flesh.*[62] Pause over the question! And oh! that a gracious God may grant you an answer of peace. If this be your portion, then need you nothing more to make you happy. For God saith to you as to the Patriarch: *I will give you the land wherein you are a stranger.*[63] And where is that, but heaven? Dearest Jesus! hast thou not taken possession of it in the name of thy people? and hast thou not promised, that *thou wilt come again and receive them to thyself, that where thou art, there they shall be also.*[64]

Poor timorous, doubting Believer! Did God say to Abraham that he would bless him, and in confirmation of it, reveal himself by this glorious name—the Almighty God; beg of him then for grace to convert this promise into a prayer: and plead, that the same God may be to thee and thine, the God all-sufficient. And oh! that every gracious soul may find grace as

62   Philippians 3:3.
63   Genesis 17:8.
64   John 14:3.

the Patriarch did, to intreat God for the *Ishmaels* of his household, the unawakened and careless around him. And may the Lord's answer be as gracious. *I have heard* thee. (Hawker, Poor Man's Old Testament Commentary: Genesis-Numbers, 70-71)

Day 59

Reading: Genesis 18

"The LORD appeared to Abraham at the oaks of Mamre ..." Genesis 18:1

How sweet were those days of primitive simplicity, when men were in the habit of enjoying intercourse of friendship with Angels. And if (as there seems great reason to suppose), one of those celestial visitors which called on Abraham, was indeed the Son of God, in an human form; what a charming evidence doth it give of favor and condescension on the part of God, and of happiness on the part of man.

But stop, my soul! pause over the thought, and remark with suitable joy and thankfulness, the far happier state of the Church in the present hour, among those highly favored saints unto whom the Lord Jesus manifests himself, *otherwise than he doth to the world.* Since those days of Abraham, the Son of God hath come down, not merely in the form, but really and truly man, and *dwelt among us.* And his gracious visits have been, not as in the earlier ages when his name was *secret,* but to every one unto whom his blessed Spirit hath made him known, and they have *seen* his glory: *the glory as of the only begotten of the Father, full of grace and truth.*[65]

In beholding the patriarch *Abraham* drawing near and pleading with God for *Sodom,* who can forbear

---

65   John 1:14.

to call to mind that precious character of the Lord Jesus; or overlook that gracious Intercessor with God for his people, *whom the Father heareth always*. My soul! never, I charge thee, forget thy Jesus, in this his High-Priestly office. Only for thy comfort recollect, that though Abraham's mediation was not successful, such can never be the issue of the Redeemer's pleading. *He ever liveth to make intercession*. And oh! the blessedness of that assurance: *he is able to save to the uttermost all that come to God* by him.[66] (Hawker, Poor Man's Old Testament Commentary: Genesis-Numbers, 75-76)

---

66   Hebrews 7:25.

Day 60

Reading: Genesis 19

"So it was, when God destroyed the cities of the plain, he remembered Abraham and brought Lot out of the middle of the upheaval ..." Genesis 19:29

My soul! do not hastily turn thine eyes of reflection from this Chapter. Behold in it the graciousness of God's mercy in the midst of judgment, and connect with it this precious assurance, in all times of prevailing corruption like this, that *the Lord knoweth how to deliver the godly out of danger* as well as *temptation.*[67] Who shall say in the present hour what nations, ripe for destruction by sin, are still preserved by the *Lots* which are dwelling among them? Who knows, or can calculate, the extent and efficacy of those prayers of the faithful, which being quickened by divine grace are heard in the divine mercy, for the suspension of the Lord's anger from breaking forth upon a guilty land! My soul! I counsel thee to seek earnestly a spirit of grace and supplication from above, that in lamenting before a throne of mercy those sins of our common nature in which I bear a part, my spirit may so earnestly wrestle with God in the Redeemer's name and righteousness, that I may find acceptance in the Beloved.

Reader! what various views of men and things, of mercy and judgment, of grace and nature, and the

---

67   2 Peter 2:9.

very different terminations between the righteous and the wicked, doth this chapter furnish. Gracious God! let it be my mercy to be called out of Sodom; to disregard the reproaches of the ungodly, and resolutely, like Lot, to bear an open testimony against them. And when in tenderness to my lingering footsteps, thou layest thy gracious hand upon me, oh! for thy quickening power in my soul also, that I may hasten to the *Zoar* of safety, even to the Lord Jesus Christ, who alone *delivereth from the wrath to come!* (Hawker, Poor Man's Old Testament Commentary: Genesis-Numbers, 81)

Day 61

Reading: Genesis 20

"Abraham said about his wife Sarah, "She is my sister ..."" Genesis 20:2

Reader! let not the greatness of Abraham's character tempt you to overlook Abraham's infirmity. Alas! what is man in his highest attainments! Had not the Patriarch lost sight that Jehovah himself was *his shield and his exceeding great reward,*[68] he need not have condescended to such a pitiful resource for the safety of his wife. God forbid, that this weakness of the Patriarch should ever be made a pretense for the sins of others, when we see how it displeased the Lord!

Surely the Holy Spirit causeth the infirmities of the faithful to be recorded, in order to teach his people that most unquestionable truth; that *there is not a just man upon earth, that doeth good and sinneth not,*[69] and to constrain the heart into the love of Jesus; whose perfect righteousness is the alone cause of justification before God. Dearest Lord! how increasingly sweet and interesting, in every renewed instance of human infirmity which I feel in myself, or meet with in others, is thy finished salvation to my view. Oh! do thou establish my soul in it more and more. Give me to see, and know that I am thine

---

68   Genesis 15:1.
69   Ecclesiastes 7:20.

in an everlasting Covenant, *which cannot be broken:* that from having committed my soul-concerns into thy hands; all my earthly interests I may safely leave at the disposal; and that *the fear of man,* as in the case of the Patriarch, *may not bring a snare.* (Hawker, Poor Man's Old Testament Commentary: Genesis-Numbers, 84)

Day 62

Reading: Genesis 21

"Sarah said, "God has made me laugh, and everyone who hears will laugh with me."" Genesis 21:6

It was far above the power of nature, and even contrary to its laws, that the aged Sarah should be honored with a son; and even so it is beyond all ordinary rules that I, a poor, helpless, undone sinner, should find grace to bear about in my soul the indwelling Spirit of the Lord Jesus. I, who once despaired, as well I might, for my nature was as dry, and withered, and barren, and accursed as a howling wilderness, even I have been made to bring forth fruit unto holiness. Well may my mouth be filled with joyous laughter, because of the singular, surprising grace which I have received of the Lord, for I have found Jesus, the promised seed, and he is mine forever. This day will I lift up psalms of triumph unto the Lord who has remembered my low estate, for "my heart rejoiceth in the Lord; mine horn is exalted in the Lord; my mouth is enlarged over mine enemies, because I rejoice in thy salvation."

I would have all those that hear of my great deliverance from hell, and my most blessed visitation from on high, laugh for joy with me. I would surprise my family with my abundant peace; I would delight my friends with my ever-increasing happiness; I would edify the Church with my grateful confessions; and even impress the world with the cheerfulness of my daily conversation. Bunyan tells us that Mercy laughed in her sleep, and no wonder when she dreamed of Jesus; my joy shall not stop short of hers while my Beloved is the theme of my daily thoughts. The Lord Jesus is a deep sea of joy: my soul shall dive therein, shall be swallowed up in the delights of his society. Sarah looked on her Isaac, and laughed with excess of rapture, and all her friends laughed with her; and thou, my soul, look on thy Jesus, and bid heaven and earth unite in thy joy unspeakable. (Spurgeon, Morning, Jun 15)

Day 63

Reading: Genesis 22

"And Abraham called the name of that place Jehovah-jireh; as it is said to this day, In the mount of the Lord it shall be seen." Genesis 22:14 (AKJV)

My soul! how many *Jehovah-Jireh's* hast thou erected? At least, how many occasions hath thy bountiful Lord afforded thee for erecting them? Oh! what cause have I to blush in the recollection! Had I done by my God as Abraham did by his, what blessed helps would they have afforded me, in the same moment that they became monuments to the Lord's praise! Surely, I know all this, in theory, very plainly and fully; but how do I fall short in the practice of it! To set up the *Jehovah-Jireh* for all that is past, is the best help to a soul in exercises for all that is to come. When I can, and do put down, after any sharp trial, my *Jehovah-Jireh*, and say, here it was "the Lord did provide," will it not, in any future exercise, enable me to say, "If the Lord helped me *then*, may I not hope that he will help me *now*?" It would be a very sad requital for past mercies, in the moment of receiving them, to say, "Alas! the Lord did once help: but he will not, I fear, do it again." This would be to read the inscription of the *Jehovah-Jireh* backward. Whereas the very sight of our *Jehovah-Jireh's* would be to say, "Here the Lord helped me— here he manifested his free unmerited grace to me;

and will he not again? Is he less Jehovah than he was? Is he not God all-sufficient, all-gracious still?" Oh! it is blessed to have such stones set up as Abraham's *Jehovah-Jireh*. There was nothing in the patriarch's of his own providing. His was simply an act of faith; and neither the result of his asking by prayer, or providing by his wisdom. And, my soul, do not overlook a most interesting mark which the Holy Spirit hath put upon Abraham's *Jehovah-Jireh*, in adding, "As it is said to this day, In the mount of the Lord it shall be seen." As if he had said, "All the ages and generations yet to come shall profit by the great father of the faithful's testimony to this place; and they shall see it to the latest day of Jesus's Church upon earth! Oh! how blessed, when our personal experience bears an exact correspondence to that of the faithful gone before, when we can and do set up the same. All blessings, all provisions are in Jesus. He is the Lamb which, from everlasting, Jehovah hath provided, and whom his people shall see in all their wants, temporal, spiritual, and eternal. And let their extremities be what they may, yea, though the exercises of their faith abound, yet let them wait but the Lord's time, which is always the best time, and they shall most assuredly, like Abraham, find cause to call the name of every place of trial *Jehovah-Jireh*; concerning which, in proof and in reality, it shall be said every day, and to the last day, "In the mount of the Lord it shall be seen!" (Hawker, The Poor Man's Evening Portion, Jul 15)

Day 64

Reading: Genesis 23

"The field with its cave passed from the Hethites to Abraham as burial property." Genesis 23:20

I detain the Reader but with *two* reflections on this Chapter. May the Holy Spirit increase them largely, and profitably to his mind! The *one* is, that in the confirmation of God's promises to Abraham, to give him Canaan for an everlasting possession, the first spot of it which he could truly call his own, was his burying-place. This was indeed possessing it, until the glorious morning of a resurrection. The *other* is, from hence the first sound of that sweet declaration was made, which *John* in after ages heard more distinctly: *Blessed are the dead which die in the Lord. These all died in faith,*[70] said the Apostle. They fell asleep in Jesus. Lord, grant me the same faith? May it be my portion that, wherever the *Macpelah* for my earthly house may be, Jesus may receive my soul: and may it be found in that hour that *I have a building with God, an house not made with hands, eternal in the heavens.*[71] (Hawker, Poor Man's Old Testament Commentary: Genesis-Numbers, 96)

---

70   Revelation 14:12-13; Hebrews 11:13.
71   2 Corinthians 5:1.

Reading: Genesis 24

"Isaac went out to meditate in the field at the eventide." Genesis 24:63 (AKJV)

Very admirable was his occupation. If those who spend so many hours in idle company, light reading, and useless pastimes, could learn wisdom, they would find more profitable society and more interesting engagements in meditation than in the vanities which now have such charms for them. We should all know more, live nearer to God, and grow in grace, if we were more alone. Meditation chews the cud and extracts the real nutriment from the mental food gathered elsewhere. When Jesus is the theme, meditation is sweet indeed. Isaac found Rebecca while engaged in private musings; many others have found their best beloved there.

Very admirable was the choice of place. In the field we have a study hung round with texts for thought. From the cedar to the hyssop, from the soaring eagle down to the chirping grasshopper, from the blue expanse of heaven to a drop of dew, all things are full of teaching, and when the eye is divinely opened, that teaching flashes upon the mind far more vividly than from written books. Our little rooms are neither so healthy, so suggestive, so agreeable, or so inspiring as the fields. Let us count nothing common or unclean, but feel that all created things point to their Maker, and the field will at once be hallowed.

Very admirable was the season. The season of sunset as it draws a veil over the day, befits that repose of the soul when earthborn cares yield to the joys of heavenly communion. The glory of the setting sun excites our wonder, and the solemnity of approaching night awakens our awe. If the business of this day will permit it, it will be well, dear reader, if you can spare an hour to walk in the field at eventide, but if not, the Lord is in the town too, and will meet with thee in thy chamber or in the crowded street. Let thy heart go forth to meet him. (Spurgeon, Morning, Aug 15)

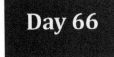

Reading: Genesis 25

"Isaac dwelt by the well Lahai-roi." Genesis 25:11 (AKJV)

Hagar had once found deliverance there and Ishmael had drunk from the water so graciously revealed by the God who liveth and seeth the sons of men; but this was a merely casual visit, such as worldlings pay to the Lord in times of need, when it serves their turn. They cry to him in trouble, but forsake him in prosperity. Isaac dwelt there, and made the well of the living and all-seeing God his constant source of supply. The usual tenor of a man's life, the dwelling of his soul, is the true test of his state. Perhaps the providential visitation experienced by Hagar struck Isaac's mind, and led him to revere the place; its mystical name endeared it to him; his frequent musings by its brim at eventide made him familiar with the well; his meeting Rebecca there had made his spirit feel at home near the spot; but best of all, the fact that he there enjoyed fellowship with the living God, had made him select that hallowed ground for his dwelling. Let us learn to live in the presence of the living God; let us pray the Holy Spirit that this day, and every other day, we may feel, "Thou God seest me." May the Lord Jehovah be as a well to us, delightful, comforting, unfailing, springing up unto eternal life. The bottle of the creature cracks and dries up, but the well of the Creator never fails; happy is he who dwells at the well, and so has abundant and constant supplies near at hand. The Lord has been a sure helper to others: his name is Shaddai, God All-sufficient; our hearts have often had most delightful intercourse with him; through him our soul has found her glorious Husband, the Lord Jesus; and in him this day we live, and move, and have our being; let us, then, dwell in closest fellowship with him. Glorious Lord, constrain us that we may never leave thee, but dwell by the well of the living God. (Spurgeon, Morning, Feb 17)

Day 67

Reading: Genesis 26

"There was another famine in the land in addition to the one that had occurred in Abraham's time ..." Genesis 26:1

Let no true believer in Jesus ever be discouraged by the trials he meets with, since the faithful in all ages have been so exercised. The Apostle makes this an evidence of the Christian character, that *no man should be moved by these afflictions, since* (saith he) *ye yourselves know that we are appointed thereunto.*[72] Oh! it is sweet to see divine wisdom, and divine faithfulness, in all appointments concerning us; and to be able to say of every one of them, as *Paul* did, *I know that this shall turn to my salvation, through the supply of the Spirit of Jesus Christ.*[73] But how very gracious is God amidst all the chequered circumstances of life, in famine, and in fullness, to renew to his people the unalterable assurances of his Covenant love in Christ Jesus! Reader! may it be your happiness and mine, to live upon this when all the supplies of creature cisterns be dried up; and like *David*, rejoice in that God hath made with us *an everlasting covenant, ordered in all things and sure;* and let this be *all our salvation, and all our desire, although he make it not to grow.*[74] I would have

---

72   1 Thessalonians 3:3.

73   Philippians 1:19.

74   2 Samuel 23:5.

the Reader, methinks, (as I desire myself) to seek grace from the Lord, to profit by what this Chapter relates of the weakness of *Isaac's* faith, respecting the safety of his wife, and of his own life, Had he only considered, poor man, the faithfulness of that God who had promised him his assured favor and protection; there was nothing in the circumstances of his situation to have given him a real cause of fear. But consulting with flesh and blood, and not laying hold of God's promises, his trust in the Lord gave way, and he fell into temptation, sin, and unbelief. Reader! let you and I mark it down among the memorandums of our hearts, that such will be the sure result in every believer's experience, when not upheld by divine strength, but left to the weakness of his own mind. Let you and I therefore pray with the apostle, that *we may be strengthened with all might according to his glorious power*, who is the alone strength of his people; for then, and not otherwise, shall we be able to act faith upon God's promises, *unto all patience and long suffering, with joyfulness.*[75] (Hawker, Poor Man's Old Testament Commentary: Genesis-Numbers, 112-113)

---

75   Colossians 1:10-12.

Reading: Genesis 27

"... I am old and do not know the day of my death ... so that I can bless you before I die." Genesis 27:2-4

How sweet and precious is it, to behold dying believers anxious to give their last testimony, to the faith of Jesus! Though the pious parents of the present age, have not, like the Patriarchs, a *prophetical* benediction respecting the coming Savior to give their children; yet have they a *parental* blessing at parting to deliver. And oh! how precious in the sight of the Lord is the death of his saints, when life is closed with such an honorable testimony.

But ought not the improper, and frequently ill-bestowed, affection of parents, in the partiality among their children, to learn from this example of Isaac, how sinful it becomes in the divine eye? Reader! let us pray for grace, that nothing short of the *covenant* blessing, may satisfy the desires of our souls. The Lord put away far from us that awful spirit of a carnal state, which, like Esau, makes light of the covenant mercies of God in Christ Jesus, and finds, like him, *no place for repentance, though it be sought even with tears.*[76] (Hawker, Poor Man's Old Testament Commentary: Genesis-Numbers, 119)

---

76   Hebrews 12:16-17.

Day 69

Reading: Genesis 28

"Look, I am with you and will watch over you wherever you go. I will bring you back to this land, for I will not leave you until I have done what I have promised you." Genesis 28:15.

Here is a promise to Jacob, and not to Jacob only, personally considered, but to Jacob's seed. For the apostle Paul was commissioned, by the Holy Spirit, to tell the church of Jesus, that we, as Isaac was, are the children of promise.[77] Hence this, like all other promises in Christ Jesus, is yea and amen.[78] Pause then, my soul, and ask thyself, What hath the Lord spoken to thee of? Hath he met with thee in Bethel, as he found Jacob? And hath he there spoken unto thee? How wilt thou know? Very plainly. Jesus hath met with thee, hath indeed spoken unto thee; if so be thou hast seen thine own unworthiness and sinfulness by nature and by practice; and if thou hast seen the King in his beauty, even Jesus, in his own glory, suitableness, and all-sufficiency, as a Savior; and inclined thine heart by his grace to believe in him, to depend upon him, and to live to him and his glory. What sayest thou, my soul, to these things? Is this promise, made to Jacob and his seed, thine? If so, live upon Jesus, and plead the fulfilment of it daily, hourly! Say to him, my soul, Lord! what hast

77   Galatians 4:28.
78   2 Corinthians 1:20.

thou spoken to me of, but mercy, pardon, peace, and grace, with all spiritual blessings, in Christ Jesus? And what have I to depend upon, or what indeed can I need more, but thy promise and the great Promiser? Yes, Lord Jesus! I do depend, I do believe. Surely, thou wilt never leave whom thou hast once loved; and therefore, thou wilt not leave me, until thou hast done that which thou hast spoken of in grace here, and wilt complete in glory hereafter. (Hawker, The Poor Man's Morning Portion, Oct 4)

Day 70

Reading: Genesis 29

"Laban answered, "It is not the custom in this place to give the younger daughter in marriage before the firstborn." Genesis 29:26

We do not excuse Laban for his dishonesty, but we scruple not to learn from the custom which he quoted as his excuse. There are some things which must be taken in order, and if we would win the second, we must secure the first. The second may be the more lovely in our eyes, but the rule of the heavenly country must stand, and the elder must be married first. For instance, many men desire the beautiful and well-favored Rachel of joy and peace in believing, but they must first be wedded to the tender-eyed Leah of repentance. Every one falls in love with happiness, and many would cheerfully serve twice seven years to enjoy it, but according to the rule of the Lord's kingdom, the Leah of real holiness must be beloved of our soul before the Rachel of true happiness can be attained. Heaven stands not first but second, and only by persevering to the end can we win a portion in it. The cross must be carried before the crown can be worn. We must follow our Lord in his humiliation, or we shall never rest with him in glory.

My soul, what sayest thou, art thou so vain as to hope to break through the heavenly rule? Dost thou hope for reward without labor, or honor without toil? Dismiss the idle expectation, and be content to take the ill-favored things for the sake of the sweet love of Jesus, which will recompense thee for all. In such a spirit, laboring and suffering, thou wilt find bitters grow sweet, and hard things easy. Like Jacob, thy years of service will seem unto thee but a few days for the love thou hast to Jesus; and when the dear hour of the wedding feast shall come, all thy toils shall be as though they had never been—an hour with Jesus will make up for ages of pain and labor.

Jesus, to win thyself so fair,
Thy cross I will with gladness bear:
Since so the rules of heaven ordain,
The first I'll wed the next to gain.

(Spurgeon, Eve, Nov 14)

Day 71

Reading: Genesis 30

It would be a far happier world than experience proves it now is, if that charming observation of the psalmist were more generally adopted, when he saith, *Lo! children are an heritage of the Lord, and the fruit of the womb is his reward.*[79] There is a blessedness pronounced upon the quiver that is full of them. And when a gracious parent beholds a rising generation of gracious children, to call the Lord blessed, when he is gathered to his fathers; the imagination can hardly form an idea of a subject more highly calculated to call forth thankfulness unto God. It is pleasing in the reflection to the upright in heart and mind, when like Jacob, in their dealings between man and man, they have the favor of the divine approbation. But what a double sweetness rests upon the possessions of the just, when every blessing is found to lead the soul *to* God, instead of drawing the heart *from* God. Lord, I would pray, that all thy mercies may be thus sanctified, and not one of them received but with thanksgiving and prayer; that coming from thy bounty, they may lead to thy praise, and all be doubly enjoyed in Jesus. (Hawker, Poor Man's Old Testament Commentary: Genesis-Numbers, 132)

---

79   Psalm 127:3.

Day 72

Reading: Genesis 31

"I could do you great harm, but last night the God of your father said to me: 'Watch yourself! Don't say anything to Jacob, either good or bad.'" Genesis 31:29

In the perusal of this Chapter, methinks I would not have the Reader overlook the gracious interposition of God, in behalf of his servant Jacob, when *Laban* the *Syrian* pursued him in such determined anger. Rather than the poor servant should be injured by his unkind, and unnatural master, the Lord overawes his mind by the effects of a dream. Just so, depend upon it, my brother, is the watchful care of God over his people now. Oh! could you and I but be brought acquainted with the thousand and ten thousand instances of the kind, which are daily going on in life, we should see how sweetly the Church's history is again, and again repeated: *he made them also to be pitied of all those that carried them captives.*[80] Reader! watch but the tokens of divine faithfulness towards *you*, in disposing the hearts of your enemies to be at peace with you, and, depend upon it, the evidences will fully appear. *In the mount of the Lord it shall be seen.*[81]

But do not close the chapter until that you have remarked with me, how continually the Patriarch's

---

80   Psalm 106:46.
81   Genesis 22:14.

history is leading us to the contemplation of the life of the blessed Jesus, of whom in numberless instances, Jacob was a type. Certainly, the Holy Spirit, in his divine ministry of glorifying Jesus, intended the records of this man's memoirs to direct us more immediately to Christ. How was Jesus obliged to flee into Egypt to avoid the fury of those that sought his life! How was he afterwards led into the wilderness! What services did he sustain for the Church, both Jew and Gentile, which he betrothed to himself! And what persecutions did he go through, in those labors of love, for the souls of his people! Dearest Lord! may a sense of thine unequalled regard to our poor fallen nature, how base so ever requited by the world, endear thee to my heart; and may it be my portion, with thy people, to have that testimony in my experience: *We love him because he first loved us!*[82] (Hawker, Poor Man's Old Testament Commentary: Genesis-Numbers, 139)

---

82   1 John 4:19.

Reading: Genesis 32

"Jacob was left alone, and a man wrestled with him until daybreak. When the man saw that he could not defeat him, he struck Jacob's hip socket as they wrestled and dislocated his hip. Then he said to Jacob, "Let me go, for it is daybreak." But Jacob said, "I will not let you go unless you bless me." Genesis 32:24-26

Never was there a conflict of so illustrious a nature, and of so strange a result, between powers so dissimilar and extreme. The incarnate God, as if to demonstrate His own Divine power, and at the same time to make the victory of human weakness over infinite might more illustrious and palpable, touches the wrestling patriarch, and he is a cripple! Then at the moment of his greatest weakness, when taught the lesson of his own insufficiency, that flesh might not glory in the Divine presence, Omnipotence retires as if vanquished from the field, and yields the palm of victory to the disabled but prevailing prince. And why all this? To teach us the amazing power of prayer, which the feeblest believer may have when alone with Jesus.

No point of Christian duty and privilege set before you in this work will plead more earnestly and tenderly for your solemn consideration, dear reader, than this. It enters into the very essence of your spiritual being. This is the channel through which flows the oil that feeds the lamp of your Christian profession. Dimly will burn that lamp, and drooping will be your spiritual light, if you are not used to be much alone with Jesus. Every feeling of the soul, and each department of Christian labor, will be sensibly affected by this woeful neglect. He who is but seldom with Jesus in the closet will exhibit, in all that he does for Jesus in the world, but the fitful and convulsive movements of a mind urged on by a feverish and unnatural excitement. It is only in much prayer-that prayer secret and confiding-that the heart is kept in its right position, its affections properly governed, and its movements correctly regulated. And are there not periods when you find it needful to leave the society of the most spiritual-sweet as is the communion of saints-to be alone with Jesus? He Himself has set you the example. Accustomed at times to withdraw from His disciples, He has been known to spend whole nights amid the mountains' solitude, alone with His Father.

Oh, the sacredness, the solemnity of such a season! Alone with God! Alone with Jesus! No eye seeing, no ear hearing, but His; the dearest of earthly being excluded, and no one present save Jesus only - the best, the dearest of all! Then, in the sweetest and most unreserved confidence, the believer unveils his soul, and reveals all to the Lord. Conscience is read – motives are dissected – principles are sifted – actions are examined – the heart is searched – sin is confessed – iniquity is acknowledged, as could only effectually be done in the presence of Jesus alone. Is there, among all the privileges of a child of God, one in its costliness and its preciousness surpassing this? (Winslow, Evening Thoughts, May 17)

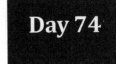

Reading: Genesis 33

"But Esau ran to meet him, hugged him, threw his arms around him, and kissed him. Then they wept." Genesis 33:4

How sweetly doth grace induce all the finer affections of the heart, and constrain all our angry passions into love! Lord, let thy grace enable us to *put on, as the elect of God, holy and beloved, bowels of mercy, kindness, humbleness of mind, meekness, long-suffering, forbearing one another, and forgiving one another, even as Christ hath forgiven us, so also may we.*[83] And in the reading of this chapter, I would beg of God to bestow, both upon him that reads, and on him that writes, the grace of having a wise choice between the fulness of this earth's blessing, and the appointment of whatever the Lord sees fit in a covenant way. Dearest Jesus! while the *Esaus* of the present hour, are sending out into the highways to enquire of every one they meet, who will shew them any good: let but *the light of thy countenance be lifted on my soul, and it will put gladness in my heart, more than in the time that corn and wine increase.*[84] (Hawker, Poor Man's Old Testament Commentary: Genesis-Numbers, 147)

---

83   Colossians 3:12-13.
84   Psalm 4:6-7.

Day 75

Reading: Genesis 34

Hitherto the Patriarch Jacob had been exercised with many sharp and trying afflictions, as they arose out of the circumstances of his own life. In this chapter, the history of the Patriarch records the beginning of the afflictions with which he was exercised, as they arose out of the circumstances of his children. *Dinah* his daughter, and as it should seem his only daughter, prompted by vain curiosity, going forth to see the daughters of the land, is ravished by *Shechem* prince of the *Hivites*. Jacob's soul is grieved at hearing of it. His sons determine to be revenged. *Hamor* the father of Shechem, in order to gratify his son's wishes, proposeth a treaty of marriage between his son and Jacob's daughter; the sons of Jacob appear to give consent, on condition of the Hivites being circumcised: but when this was done, Simeon and Levi come upon their city by surprise, destroy all the males, and take away their cattle. (Hawker, Poor Man's Old Testament Commentary: Genesis-Numbers, 148)

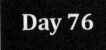

Day 76

Reading: Genesis 35

"She called his name Benoni (son of sorrow), but his father called him Benjamin (son of my right hand)." Genesis 35:18 (AKJV)

To every matter there is a bright as well as a dark side. Rachel was overwhelmed with the sorrow of her own travail and death; Jacob, though weeping the mother's loss, could see the mercy of the child's birth. It is well for us if, while the flesh mourns over trials, our faith triumphs in divine faithfulness. Samson's lion yielded honey, and so will our adversities, if rightly considered. The stormy sea feeds multitudes with its fishes; the wild wood blooms with beauteous florets; the stormy wind sweeps away the pestilence, and the biting frost loosens the soil. Dark clouds distil bright drops, and black earth grows gay flowers. A vein of good is to be found in every mine of evil. Sad hearts have peculiar skill in discovering the most disadvantageous point of view from which to gaze upon a trial; if there were only one slough in the world, they would soon be up to their necks in it, and if there were only one lion in the desert they would hear it roar. About us all there is a tinge of this wretched folly, and we are apt, at times, like Jacob, to cry, "All these things are against me."[85] Faith's way of walking is to cast all care upon the Lord, and then to anticipate good results from the worst calamities.

85   Genesis 42:36.

Like Gideon's men, she does not fret over the broken pitcher, but rejoices that the lamp blazes forth the more. Out of the rough oyster-shell of difficulty she extracts the rare pearl of honor, and from the deep ocean-caves of distress she uplifts the priceless coral of experience. When her flood of prosperity ebbs, she finds treasures hid in the sands; and when her sun of delight goes down, she turns her telescope of hope to the starry promises of heaven. When death itself appears, faith points to the light of resurrection beyond the grave, thus making our dying Benoni to be our living Benjamin. (Spurgeon, Eve, Mar 8)

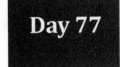

Reading: Genesis 36

"... Esau was father of the Edomites." Genesis 36:43

There is much spiritual improvement to be drawn from the perusal of this Chapter by every gracious soul, when God the Holy Spirit awakens the heart to the observation. *Jacob's* seed, no doubt, while they were bond-slaves in *Egypt* felt their misery the more, while calling to mind the splendor of Esau's race in *Edom*. But how mistaken are our views of things, and what false calculations do we make in our estimation of happiness. Esau's children were great indeed among men. But the seed of Jacob were beloved in the sight of God. Jesus hath made them *kings and priests to God and the Father, and they shall reign with him forever.*[86] Dear Lord! give me that sweet promise and I ask no more. *To him that overcometh will I grant to sit with me on my throne.*[87] (Hawker, Poor Man's Old Testament Commentary: Genesis-Numbers, 161)

---

86   Revelation 1:6; 20:6; 2 Timothy 2:12.
87   Revelation 3:21.

Day 78

Reading: Genesis 37

"They sent the robe of many colors to their father and said, "We found this. Examine it. Is it your son's robe or not?" His father recognized it. "It is my son's robe," he said ..." Genesis 37:32-33

The life of the patriarch Joseph is very beautiful and interesting, as a history only; and the several incidents arising out of it are such as cannot but more or less affect every heart. But when we have gone through the whole relation, in the mere letter of the word, we are constrained to believe, that in the spiritual sense and meaning of it, almost everything in the life of Joseph was typical of Jesus. I would not strain scripture upon any account. Neither would I frame to myself anything fanciful of Jesus, and his blessed offices; so as to see him where he is not. But I cannot but think, that since in so many instances, as is universally allowed, Joseph is a lively type of Christ, the Holy Spirit, in his glorifying the Lord Jesus, was, in many cases, pleased to shadow forth somewhat of the Redeemer where he is not at first so immediately discovered. Whether in the passage I have just read, for the present evening's meditation, there be any thing typical of Jesus, I know not; but to those who, like Philip, have "found him of whom Moses in the law and the prophets did write, Jesus of Nazareth,"[88]—the coat of the patriarch, dipped

88   John 1:45.

in the blood of the kid, may minister in leading the heart to the contemplation of Jesus, who appeareth unceasingly in his priestly garments, in the presence of God our Father, for us. And may not a believer humbly take up the language of faith, when drawing nigh to our God and Father in Christ Jesus; and when we enter, as it were, into his retirings, with earnest prayer, and earnest pleadings, seeking favor in and through Jesus, may we not in the arms of our faith bring the vesture of Jesus dipped in blood, and say, This have we found; know now, whether it be Jesus's, thy dear and ever blessed Son's vesture, or no? Oh! for faith to behold Christ, as the Father beheld him, when he set him forth to the Church; and to love him as God our Father loved him. And how surely will God confirm his own gracious testimony concerning him, and say, as the patriarch, or in words to the same effect: This is my beloved Son, in whom I am well pleased! (Hawker, The Poor Man's Evening Portion, Feb 7)

Day 79

Reading: Genesis 38

What hath sin wrought in all ages! What a dreadful bias to evil is naturally in the mind of every man! What awful examples doth the Lord sometimes proclaim, in punishments, of his utter displeasure of sin! But, my soul! while thou art seeking grace from God, to avoid every appearance of sin, let that state of humbleness, that astonishing and unequalled state of humbleness, to which Jesus submitted, when he came to do away sin by the sacrifice of himself, endear the Redeemer yet more and more to thy heart, and form him there *the only hope of glory*.[89] Was it not enough, dearest Lord, when thou condescendest to take flesh and blood for the purposes of salvation, that thou didst not abhor the virgin's womb, but didst even appoint thine ancestors, after the flesh, to be such as were more particularly marked with unworthiness? Gracious Redeemer! may it serve to teach my heart those sweet lessons, that thou wert pleased to be made in all things like as we are, yet without sin: and although thou wert made in the *likeness* of sinful flesh, yet thou didst partake of none of the corruptions of flesh; and that in thy tender alliance with our nature, thou dost not refuse that alliance even with the vilest of our nature; but *where sin aboundeth, grace doth much more abound; that as sin hath reigned unto death, even so might*

89   Colossians 1:27.

grace reign through righteousness, unto eternal life, by Jesus Christ our Lord.[90] (Hawker, Poor Man's Old Testament Commentary: Genesis-Numbers, 170)

---

90   Romans 5:20-21.

Day 80

Reading: Genesis 39

"... But leaving his garment in her hand, he escaped and ran outside." Genesis 39:12

In contending with certain sins there remains no mode of victory but by flight. The ancient naturalists wrote much of basilisks, whose eyes fascinated their victims and rendered them easy victims; so, the mere gaze of wickedness puts us in solemn danger. He who would be safe from acts of evil must haste away from occasions of it. A covenant must be made with our eyes not even to look upon the cause of temptation, for such sins only need a spark to begin with and a blaze follows in an instant. Who would wantonly enter the leper's prison and sleep amid its horrible corruption? He only who desires to be leprous himself would thus court contagion. If the mariner knew how to avoid a storm, he would do anything rather than run the risk of weathering it. Cautious pilots have no desire to try how near the quicksand they can sail, or how often they may touch a rock without springing a leak; their aim is to keep as nearly as possible in the midst of a safe channel.

This day I may be exposed to great peril, let me have the serpent's wisdom to keep out of it and avoid it. The wings of a dove may be of more use to me today than the jaws of a lion. It is true I may be an apparent loser by declining evil company, but I had better leave my cloak than lose my character; it is not needful that I should be rich, but it is imperative upon me to be pure. No ties of friendship, no chains of beauty, no flashings of talent, no shafts of ridicule must turn me from the wise resolve to flee from sin. The devil I am to resist and he will flee from me, but the lusts of the flesh, I must flee, or they will surely overcome me. O God of holiness preserve thy Josephs, that Madam Bubble bewitch them not with her vile suggestions. May the horrible trinity of the world, the flesh, and the devil, never overcome us! (Spurgeon, Morning, Jul 25)

Day 81

Reading: Genesis 40

"Then Joseph said to them, "Don't interpretations belong to God? Tell me your dreams."" Genesis 40:8

Reader! mark this down in the memorandums of your life, that whether in a prison or a palace, the faithful have God for their portion. And what a sweet thought is it, that, as no walls can confine the souls of God's people; so neither can bolts or bars shut the Lord out. If you are the Lord's prisoner, this is preferable to being the world's freeman. And when we recollect how precious the enjoyments some have found in those seasons, very evident it is that the Comforter is with them, and that to bless them. But even here in Joseph's history, let me not lose sight of the Lord Jesus, who *was taken from prison and from judgment, and who shall declare his generation?* Blessed Lord! let me never forget the afflictions of my spiritual and almighty Joseph, nor the cause of them; but in all events of life as well prosperous as distressing, cease not to remember thee! (Hawker, Poor Man's Old Testament Commentary: Genesis-Numbers, 177)

Reading: Genesis 41

"The ill-favored and lean fleshed kine [cows] did eat up the seven well-favored and fat kine [cows] ..."
Genesis 41:4 (AKJV)

Pharaoh's dream has too often been my waking experience. My days of sloth have ruinously destroyed all that I had achieved in times of zealous industry; my seasons of coldness have frozen all the genial glow of my periods of fervency and enthusiasm; and my fits of worldliness have thrown me back from my advances in the divine life. I had need to beware of lean prayers, lean praises, lean duties, and lean experiences, for these will eat up the fat of my comfort and peace. If I neglect prayer for never so short a time, I lose all the spirituality to which I had attained; if I draw no fresh supplies from heaven, the old corn in my granary is soon consumed by the famine which rages in my soul. When the caterpillars of indifference, the cankerworms of worldliness, and the palmerworms of self-indulgence, lay my heart completely desolate, and make my soul to languish, all my former fruitfulness and growth in grace avails me nothing whatever. How anxious should I be to have no lean-fleshed days, no ill-favored hours! If every day I journeyed towards the goal of my desires I should soon reach it, but backsliding leaves me still far off from the prize of my high calling, and robs me of the advances which I had so laboriously made. The only way in which all my days can be as the "fat kine," is to feed them in the right meadow, to spend them with the Lord, in His service, in His company, in His fear, and in His way. Why should not every year be richer than the past, in love, and usefulness, and joy? – I am nearer the celestial hills, I have had more experience of my Lord, and should be more like Him. O Lord, keep far from me the curse of leanness of soul; let me not have to cry, "My leanness, my leanness, woe unto me!" but may I be well-fed and nourished in thy house, that I may praise thy name. (Spurgeon, Morning, Jul 3)

Reading: Genesis 42

"Although Joseph recognized his brothers, they did not recognize him." Genesis 42:8

This morning our desires went forth for growth in our acquaintance with the Lord Jesus; it may be well tonight to consider a kindred topic, namely, our heavenly Joseph's knowledge of us. This was most blessedly perfect long before we had the slightest knowledge of him. "His eyes beheld our substance, yet being imperfect, and in his book all our members were written, when as yet there was none of them." Before we had a being in the world, we had a being in his heart. When we were enemies to him, he knew us, our misery, our madness, and our wickedness. When we wept bitterly in despairing repentance, and viewed him only as a judge and a ruler, he viewed us as his brethren well beloved, and his bowels yearned towards us. He never mistook his chosen, but always beheld them as objects of his infinite affection. "The Lord knoweth them that are his,"[91] is as true of the prodigals who are feeding swine as of the children who sit at the table.

But, alas! we knew not our royal Brother, and out of this ignorance grew a host of sins. We withheld our hearts from him, and allowed him no entrance to our love. We mistrusted him, and gave no credit

---

91   2 Timothy 2:19.

to his words. We rebelled against him, and paid him no loving homage. The Sun of Righteousness shone forth, and we could not see him. Heaven came down to earth, and earth perceived it not. Let God be praised, those days are over with us; yet even now it is but little that we know of Jesus compared with what he knows of us. We have but begun to study him, but he knoweth us altogether. It is a blessed circumstance that the ignorance is not on his side, for then it would be a hopeless case for us. He will not say to us, "I never knew you,"[92] but he will confess our names in the day of his appearing, and meanwhile will manifest himself to us as he doth not unto the world. (Spurgeon, Eve, Jan 4)

---

92   Matthew 7:23.

Reading: Genesis 43

"Now the famine in the land was severe. When they had used up the grain they had brought back from Egypt, their father said to them, "Go back and buy us a little food."" Genesis 43:1-2

R eader! let you and I turn from the table of Joseph amidst his brethren, while they are thus merry and happy with him, to consider the spiritual interest which we have in these things.

The world which we dwell in, like that of Canaan to the Patriarch's family, is a world of famine in bread for the soul. And if you know what spiritual hunger means, you will know also that this heavenly corn for ourselves and our household, can nowhere else be had but of the lord of the country, even from the Lord Jesus; of whom Joseph was the type. Shall we not arise and go to him? We will not, like Jacob's sons, take a present in our hand, for he is too rich to be benefitted by our favors: and his blessings are too great to come within the price of purchase. But like Jacob, let us pray that God Almighty may give us mercy before the *man,* even the God-man Christ Jesus.

Dearest Lord, behold us now before thee! Oh! say to thy stewards the ministers of thy table as Joseph did to his: *bring these men home and make ready, for these men shall dine with me at noon.* And oh!

the wonderful condescension, Jesus indeed *receiveth sinners and eateth with them.*[93] We see thy face. We behold thy glory. We hear thy voice. We rejoice and are merry like the brethren of Joseph, while our brother Jesus saith, *Eat, O friends; drink, yea, drink abundantly, O beloved.*[94] And dearest Redeemer! we would pray do thou make our meeting gracious in drawing nigh to us by thy Holy Spirit, in opening to our minds the Holy Scriptures, and in making thyself known to us in breaking of bread and in prayer. Then shall we fully understand and have our souls refreshed indeed in the experience, *that thy flesh is meat indeed, and thy blood drink indeed.*[95] (Hawker, Poor Man's Old Testament Commentary: Genesis-Numbers, 194-195)

---

93 Luke 15:2.
94 Song of Songs / Solomon 5:1.
95 John 6:55.

Reading: Genesis 44

"... The man in whose possession the cup was found will be my slave ..." Genesis 44:17

This Chapter opens to our view very profitable reflections. How soon was the joy of the children of Israel turned into mourning. And yet in the midst of both, their covenant God was carrying on one and the same plan of mercy towards them. Learn, my soul, in all the checquered circumstances of life to remember this, and both in prosperity and adversity to live upon an unchangeable God.

But chiefly let this Chapter, with all the events of it, lead me to Jesus. Whatever tends to detain me, or to bring me back to him, may I esteem a mercy! Dearest Lord! put thou the cup of salvation in my lot, and may it be my portion to be thy servant forever. I would cry unto thee as one of old; *Give ear, O shepherd of Israel, thou that leadest Joseph like a flock; thou that dwellest between the cherubims shine forth. Before Ephraim, and Benjamin, and Manasseh, stir up thy strength, and come, and save us. Turn us again, O God, and cause thy face to shine, and we shall be saved.*[96] (Hawker, Poor Man's Old Testament Commentary: Genesis-Numbers, 199)

---

96   Psalm 80:1-3.

Day 86

Reading: Genesis 45

"'Do this: Take wagons from the land of Egypt for your dependents and your wives and bring your father here. Do not be concerned about your belongings, for the best of all the land of Egypt is yours.'" Genesis 45:19-20

How grateful, after afflictions, are the renewals of joy! How refreshing the manifestations of Jesus after long, and dark seasons of his absence to the soul? Reader! let the perusal of this Chapter be sure to lead thy heart to the examination, whether Jesus hath made himself known to thee otherwise than he doth to the world. For without this the chief and best improvement from it will be lost. Oh! it is sweet to look at him whom by sin and disobedience we have sold for a slave! It is precious, indeed, to behold him who was wounded for our sins and bruised for our iniquities; now risen and exalted at the right hand of power; and though changed in state, yet still retaining the same nature, and still not ashamed to call his people Brethren.

Dearest Jesus! send the wagons of thine ordinances to bring us to thyself. Into the Egypt of even death and the grave would we follow thee, to behold thy glory. And as the good of all the land is before us, and in the heaven into which thou art entered, thou art only gone before as our fore-runner to take possession in our name; thither may thy good Spirit bring us, as to our eternal home: where we hope to see thee *face to face, and to know even as we are known.*[97] (Hawker, Poor Man's Old Testament Commentary: Genesis-Numbers, 203)

---

97   1 Corinthians 13:12.

Day 87

Day 87

Reading: Genesis 46

"... Do not be afraid to go down to Egypt, for I will make you into a great nation there. I will go down with you to Egypt, and I will also bring you back ..."
Genesis 46:3-4

Jacob must have shuddered at the thought of leaving the land of his father's sojourning, and dwelling among heathen strangers. It was *a new scene, and likely to be a trying one*: who shall venture among couriers of a foreign monarch without anxiety? Yet the way was *evidently appointed* for him, and therefore he resolved to go. This is frequently the position of believers now—they are called to perils and temptations altogether untried: at such seasons *let them imitate Jacob's example* by offering sacrifices of prayer unto God, and seeking his direction; let them not take a step until they have waited upon the Lord for his blessing: then they *will have Jacob's companion* to be their friend and helper. How blessed to feel assured that the Lord is with us in all our ways, and condescends to go down into our humiliations and banishments with us! Even beyond the ocean our Father's love beams like the sun in its strength. We cannot hesitate to go where Jehovah promises his presence; even the valley of death-shade grows bright with the radiance of this assurance. Marching onwards with faith in their God, believers *shall have Jacob's promise*. They shall be brought up again, whether it be from the troubles of life or the chambers of death. Jacob's seed came out of Egypt in due time, and so shall all the faithful pass unscathed through the tribulation of life, and the terror of death. Let us *exercise Jacob's confidence.* "*Fear not,*" is the Lord's command and his divine encouragement to those who at his bidding are launching upon new seas; the divine presence and preservation forbid so much as one unbelieving fear. Without our God we should fear to move; but when he bids us to, it would be dangerous to tarry. Reader, go forward, and fear not. (Spurgeon, Eve, May 12)

Day 88

Reading: Genesis 47

"My years have been few and hard." Genesis 47:9

What sweet lessons do the lives of the Patriarchs Jacob and Joseph afford, of endearing ties of parental and filial affection? Would we learn the influence of grace refining nature's feelings, let us read over those sacred records.

Reader! do not forget to spiritualize the Egyptian monarch's question to the hoary Patriarch, and ask the same of your own heart. How old are you in grace? What years, what days can you number since you were new born? Few and evil no doubt are the best of our days in the best of our pilgrimage. But do not forget that the spiritual arithmetic is not counted by natural calculations: *for the child of grace shall die an hundred years old; but the sinner* still remaining in an unconverted, unrenewed state, *being an hundred years old shall be accursed.*[98]

From the tender affection of Joseph to his dying father, in the promise he made him, let me turn my eyes and contemplate Joseph's Lord and Savior in the promise he hath left to all his people. He saith to all the true spiritual seed of Israel now, as to the Patriarch himself; *Fear not to go down to the grave, I will be with thee.* And this thought is a sweet thought: the covenant holds good in death as in life. The grave

---

98   Isaiah 65:20.

cannot dissolve it. When *we live, we live unto the Lord: and when we die, we die unto the Lord: so that living or dying we are the Lord's.*[99] O thou that hast the keys of hell and death; sweetest Saviour! be thou my God, my guide and my companion, both in life and in death: then *to live will be Christ, and to die will be gain.*[100] (Hawker, Poor Man's Old Testament Commentary: Genesis-Numbers, 212)

99   Romans 14:8.
100   Philippians 1:21.

Day 89

Reading: Genesis 48

"... the God who has been my shepherd all my life to this day," Genesis 48:15

Reader! I would pass by many very sweet and interesting reflections which arise out of this Chapter, to fix my mind upon one most eminently striking, and as important as it is striking: namely, how triumphant must be that glorious principle of faith which animated the Patriarch's mind at such a distant period before the coming of Jesus; and which enabled him to sing such a song of praise *to the God which had fed him all his life long, and to the angel which redeemed him from all evil.* Oh, my soul! if these all died in faith in a *coming* savior; shall not I, now I have seen him *come;* having *finished transgression, made an end of sin, made reconciliation for iniquity, brought in an everlasting righteousness, and sealed up the vision:*[101] shall not I find grace to be *the follower of them, who now through faith and patience inherit the promises?*[102] Blessed Lord! give me this precious gift of faith. Enable me to see God's Christ in this great salvation; and by an ardent lively faith to know my right of appropriation in it. Then shall I be assured, even as Jacob was in a dying hour, that *this God is my God for ever and ever, and he will be my guide even unto death.* (Hawker, Poor Man's Old Testament Commentary: Genesis-Numbers, 216)

101	Daniel 9:24.
102	Hebrews 6:12.

Reading: Genesis 49

"Yet his bow remained steady, and his strong arms were made agile by the hands of the Mighty One of Jacob, ..." Genesis 49:24

That strength which God gives to his Josephs is *real* strength; it is not a boasted valor, a fiction, a thing of which men talk, but which ends in smoke; it is true—*divine strength*. Why does Joseph stand against temptation? Because God gives him aid. There is naught that we can do without the power of God. All true strength comes from "the mighty God of Jacob." Notice in what a *blessedly familiar way* God gives this strength to Joseph – "The arms of his hands were made strong by the hands of the mighty God of Jacob." Thus, God is represented as putting his hands on Joseph's hands, placing his arms on Joseph's arms. Like as a father teaches his children, so the Lord teaches them that fear him. He puts his arms upon them. Marvelous condescension! God Almighty, Eternal, Omnipotent, stoops from his throne and lays his hand upon the child's hand, stretching his arm upon the arm of Joseph, that he may be made strong! This strength was also covenant strength, for it is ascribed to "the mighty *God of Jacob*." Now, wherever you read of the God of Jacob in the Bible, you should remember the covenant with Jacob. Christians love to think of God's covenant.

All the power, all the grace, all the blessings, all the mercies, all the comforts, all the things we have, flow to us from the well-head, through the covenant. If there were no covenant, then we should fail indeed; for all grace proceeds from it, as light and heat from the sun. No angels ascend or descend, save upon that ladder which Jacob saw, at the top of which stood a covenant God. Christian, it may be that the archers have sorely grieved you, and shot at you, and wounded you, but still your bow abides in strength; be sure, then, to ascribe all the glory to Jacob's God. (Spurgeon, Morning, Feb 22)

Day 91

Reading: Genesis 50

"You planned evil against me; God planned it for good to bring about the present result—the survival of many people." Genesis 50:20

Reader! it would be wrong to close our review of the life of the Patriarch Joseph, without once more looking at so illustrious a character, both as he is in himself, and as he is a type of the ever-blessed Jesus. As he is in himself, how truly lovely doth he appear in every relation and character of life. As a son, as a brother, as the wise governor in Egypt, raised up by the Lord for the preservation of his own house and family, and the whole kingdom of Egypt. And as a father, as a man, when a servant, and when a Lord! But how lovely is it to see the Holy Spirit graciously shadowing out the features of Jesus, in the prominent parts of Joseph's life. From the first departure he made from his father's house, through the whole of his eventful life, from the prison to the throne, we see the outlines of the great Redeemer's history sketched out. And from Joseph we are immediately directed to Jesus, and as we bow the knee before him, we cannot help crying out; Hail! thou glorious Almighty Governor of thy kingdom! Thou art indeed the true *Zapnath-paaneah.* Thou art He whom thy brethren shall praise, and all thy church adore. To thee every knee shall bow, and every tongue confess that thou art Christ, to the glory of God the Father.

Before we shut this book of Genesis let us take one thought more. The close of it may lead our minds to the improving thought of the close of our own. It serves to enforce upon the mind that solemn conclusion of the sacred writer; *so teach us to number our days that we may apply our hearts unto wisdom.*[103] Reader! what a vast change hath been wrought in the circumstances of mankind, from the opening of the history of creation through the several periods of it. *There* we began the wonderful relation of God's goodness to our race, in the formation of man after his own image. And *here* we behold him become the prey and food of worms! And whence all this but because *sin hath entered into the world, and death by sin: and so death hath passed upon all men, because all have sinned.*[104] And what shall bring relief to the mind under this discouraging prospect, but the contemplation of his love and faithfulness, who is the unchangeable covenant God, *the same yesterday and today and forever.*[105] Reader! may it be your happiness and mine, to live upon this great and unchangeable God, as he is revealed to his people in a three-fold character of persons. And under this assurance that blessing will be our portion: *the children of thy servants shall continue, and their seed shall be established before thee.* (Hawker, Poor Man's Old Testament Commentary: Genesis-Numbers, 224–225)

---

103   Psalm 90:12.
104   Romans 5:12.
105   Hebrews 13:8.

Works Cited

- 2017. *Christian Standard Bible.* Nashville, TN: Holman Bible Publishers.

- Hawker, Robert. 1805. *The Poor Man's Commentary on the Bible: Genesis-Deuteronomy.* Vol. 1. London.*

- —. 1805. *The Poor Man's Commentary on the Bible: Job-Psalms.* Vol. 4. London.*

- —. 1845. *The Poor Man's Evening Portion.* A New Edition. Philadelphia: Thomas Wardle.*

- —. 1845. *The Poor Man's Morning Portion.* Pittsburg: Robert Carter.*

- Spurgeon, C. H. 1896. *Morning and Evening: Daily readings.* London: Passmore & Alabaster.*

- Winslow, Octavius. 1856. *Evening Thoughts.* Leamington, England.*

- —. 1856. *Morning Thoughts.* Leamington, England.*

* = *work is in the public domain*

Author's Biographical Information

Robert Hawker (1753–1827)

Robert Hawker, a Royal Marine assistant surgeon, Anglican priest, and author, was born 1753 in Exeter, England. He was married aged 19 to Anna Rains, and they had eight children altogether. He was ordained as a minister in 1779. It was in the pulpit that "the Doctor" was best known and loved. Thousands flocked to hear the "Star of the West" preach when he was in London. An Evangelical, he preached the Bible and proclaimed the love of God. (Wikipedia: Robert Hawker 2020)

Charles H. Spurgeon (1834-1892)

Charles Haddon Spurgeon, an English Particular Baptist preacher and author, was born on 19 June 1834 in Kelvedon, Essex, England. He married Susannah Thompson in 1832 and had twin boys. Spurgeon remains highly influential among Christians of various denominations, among whom he is known as the "Prince of Preachers." (Wikipedia: Charles Spurgeon 2020)

Octavius Winslow (1808-1878)

Octavius Winslow, a pastor and author, was born on 1 August 1808 in Pentonville, a village near London. In 1834 he married Hannah Ann Ring and had ten children with her. He pastored churches in both America and England, spending most of his life in England. He was also known as "The Pilgrim's Companion," and was a prominent 19th-century evangelical preacher in England and America. (Wikipedia: Octavius Winslow 2020)

CPSIA information can be obtained
at www.ICGtesting.com
Printed in the USA
FSHW022116100720
71627FS